What Doesn't Kill You

The Lyle Bauer Story

By Robert Allan Young

    ISBN 978-1-7750340-0-1
        1.   Biography & Autobiography
        2.   Sports

Printed in Canada

Not only that, but we also boast in our sufferings, knowing that suffering produces endurance, endurance produces character, and character produces hope.
Romans 5:3

What Doesn't Kill You

Dedications

This book has been some time in the making, but I'm hoping the stories, struggles, and victories remain long after the last page is read.

This book is dedicated to my teammates.

My brothers on the grid iron, the staff, board members, and great volunteers I had the privilege of serving with.

To my cancer team; the medical providers, my brothers and sisters who have fought the battle and from whom I have gained so much respect. Also to the fabulous volunteers who make the difference in the lives of others on a daily basis.

We will continue this fight. We will fight until we can't and then, like any great team, others will step in and march forward.

Our conviction is steadfast. Our path to victory is clear and our commitment to each other is sincere.

Hope is not a method, and failure is not an option.

Lyle Bauer

To Lisa, my reader, my best friend and my love. This wouldn't have come together without your unwavering support. And to my three sons; Adam, Kevin and Marc.

Robert Allan Young

Table of Contents

Introduction

If you are reading this, I must admit that I am humbled and honored that you have taken the time to join me in this journey.

It was never my intention to put a book together, but then again, it certainly was never my intention to get cancer. No one ever asks for that.

My journey and story is in many ways similar to others who have walked the same path.

But even without cancer, my journey has been a fight and maybe that in itself has been a blessing for what has transpired later in my life.

Hopefully, through this book you will get to know me. It is important that we lay the foundation for hope, inspiration, and a coming together in the fight against a disease that has and will continue to affect one out of every three people in the future.

I have so many people to thank for what has transpired in my life and I hope the chapters of the book will pay tribute to some of them.

When I decided that this book would be the right thing to do to carry the message of the Never Alone Foundation and support the patients and families who fight cancer, it was important to find the right author. I needed someone who understood the pain, the struggle, the fight, and losses that sometimes come from personal tragedy.

I met Robert Allan Young several years ago and in addition to being an accomplished best-selling author, I knew of the personal struggles he had endured with the loss of his son, Adam, during the Winnipeg Flood of 1997.

Robert found a way for you to get to know me as a person, husband, father, friend, teammate, and cancer survivor in some of the most intimate stories of my life that have never been shared publicly.

I also have to thank my teammates and CFL brothers from other teams, as they are all contributors to what I have become and I appreciate their friendship and love as we all move further in this journey we call life.

I owe a great deal to the fabulous staff, volunteers, and supporters at the Never Alone Foundation, especially Shirlee Preteau who has been there since the inception and was there during my fight with cancer. They are the ones who truly make a difference in the lives of others with their dedication, compassion, and endless hours in support of the mission of the Never Alone Foundation. As I tell them frequently "I am just the pretty face who happened to get cancer."

I also want to recognize the great medical practitioners who saved my life and also to those who dedicate their lives in the pursuit of potential cures for cancer. They have spent decades making these strides and sacrifice a lot personally and professionally in this pursuit.

Last but not least I have to thank my wife, Heidi and our kids, Danni, Brodie, and Wesley. In addition to being my biggest supporters, they are also my main purpose in fighting on so many fronts.

Heidi has shown this kid from a broken home what true love is, the importance of family, and instilled a sense of faith that I really never had before. She has been the rock that is firmly entrenched in our values and beliefs and without her, there would be no "me". I owe her everything and hopefully that can be conveyed somewhat in the pages of this book. If there happens to be tear stains on the pages I hope you will understand.

I do believe that we are all here for a purpose however that purpose is for us to discover and pursue to the best of our abilities. Our journeys will be varied in toughness, but God selects the toughest for the difficult learning experiences.

Our lives are not defined by what we have or who we are. Our lives are defined by the difference we make in the lives of others and in making the world a better place to live, love, and learn in preparation for what is to come, whatever that may be.

Cancer has afforded me the opportunity to meet some of the most amazing and courageous people in the world. Most are not celebrities or extremely wealthy or successful. They are people that truly embrace life and will fight for every ounce of it so they can continue to create memories and experiences.

As I have said many times in the past, it is the creation of those memories that make us immortal. Memories are what live on in the minds and hearts of others long after we have passed and left this world.

In reading this book I hope that you will laugh, cry, get angry, but mostly, inspired. My hope is that you'll know who I am and that you would be a different person after you turn the last page.

In spite of everything that goes on in the world, it is a great place to be and I have been blessed on so many fronts.

There's a quote by Paul Shane Spear that says; "As one person I cannot change the world, but I can change the world of one person".

That is the spirit of the Never Alone Foundation. All those little things we do build into the bigger things that can have a profound impact on the lives of others.

This journey has not been an easy one and it continues to be a fight on many fronts.

The objective in the writing of this book is to hopefully provide inspiration and hope for so many that are walking in similar footsteps and for those who will take the journey in the future.

The cancer journey affects not only the patient, but the family and friends that come along side. They feel the pain. They feel the suffering, and in too many cases, they are the ones left to pick up the pieces in the end.

Cancer is a brutal disease that knows no bounds. It doesn't care who you are, what you do, the colour of your skin, your religion, or your sexual orientation. It is a formidable foe but we will continue the fight until the day that cancer is deemed a chronic ailment instead of a terminal disease.

The net proceeds from the sales of this book will go to the Never Alone Foundation in support of our programming that we believe makes the journey just a little easier for so many.

In addition, we will also contribute to the CFLAA (Canadian Football League Alumni Association) Support Fund in an effort to support former players and their families who require assistance in their cancer fight.

With that, it is time for "Kick Off!" As I once stated in a sports interview prior to a game, "Buckle up, Buttercup, cuz you are going on a ride like you have never seen!"

Never Alone,

Lyle Bauer

Chapter One

Have you ever noticed that something peculiar happens to us when it comes to our sports idols? We watch them on 46 inch plasma flat screens in the comfort of our homes or at neighbourhood sports bars while they sweat it out on the court, the field or the ice.

We spend hours scouring the headlines and looking for mentions about them either online or in the papers. We follow their Twitter feeds and Instagram accounts. We like their Facebook pages and add their highlight videos to our Favourites on YouTube.

Some people go even further by studying and memorizing their favourite player's statistics in such depth that they can recite them easier than our own phone number. On rare occasions, we get the opportunity to shake their hand and possibly exchange a few words. And from all that, we presume to know them.

Take for example the legendary Winnipeg Blue Bomber, #59, Lyle Bauer, a charismatic leader and tenacious competitor well known for playing through injuries and leaving it all on the field. In a career spanning 10 years in the CFL, #59 was a sports icon in Winnipeg. He became a role model and a celebrity during a stretch of some of the best football years in Winnipeg Blue Bombers' history.

Bauer was a divisional all-star and the club's top lineman in 1988. He helped his team capture three Grey Cup Championships in 1984, 1988 and 1990, and was inducted into the Winnipeg Blue Bombers Hall of Fame in 1998.

He hung up his pads, helmet and knee braces after the 1991 season and moved into the Blue Bomber's front office as the team's assistant general manager.

Bauer left the Blue Bombers in 1995 to pursue business opportunities in the grain industry, working for AgPro in Calgary, where he served as the company's General Manager.

In 2000, Bauer returned to the Winnipeg Football Club, taking over the management of the organization. As President and Chief Executive Officer, his innovative strategies in debt reduction and fundraising helped lift the Winnipeg Football Club out from under a $5-million debt and set the organization up to became a model example for the entire league.

The Winnipeg Blue Bombers made the postseason seven of the ten seasons Bauer was at the helm and the team advanced to the Grey Cup in 2001 and 2007. The club hosted five playoff games and one Grey Cup during Bauer's tenure.

He left the Winnipeg Football Club in 2010 with a record of 90-88-2, moving on to lead the Calgary Stampeders. He spent three years as President and COO of that club.

It's evident that Lyle Bauer has made a significant impact both on and off the football field since being drafted in 1979. His resume is impressive. It's interesting. It's intriguing. But it means nothing.

Because the reality is that we never really know our sports heroes as much as we would like to think. We only see a façade, the parts that they allow us to see. When it comes to sports heroes and celebrities in general, what we really should be doing is trying to understand what makes that person tick and how they have become the people they are today. Sometimes it's a classic "Glory Road" story while others tell a dark tale.

It was a cold Saturday afternoon in October 1991 at the old Winnipeg Stadium on Maroons Road. With the game still up for grabs, the Winnipeg Blue Bombers faced a second and long against their East Division rivals, the Hamilton Tiger-Cats. The sold-out crowd watched as David Black, Bob Molle, Steve Rodehutskors, Chris Walby and Lyle Bauer broke away from the huddle and set their positions at the line of scrimmage. In unison, Molle, Walby, Rodehutskors and Black bent into their three-point stances and dug their cleats into the turf. Bauer, the team's center, scanned the entire Tiger-Cats defensive formation before setting himself in position above the ball.

Quarterback Tom Burgess stepped in behind him and viewed the field while running back Robert Mimbs and fullback Matt Pearce lined up behind him in what is called an "I" formation. Burgess barked the signals and, with precise timing, Bauer lifted the ball off the turf and into this quarterback's hands. The legendary O-Line stood their ground ready for battle. But before Burgess could hand the ball off to his running back, he was lying face down in the cold turf.

Walby, angry, but mostly embarrassed, pulled himself off the field, ripped out his mouth guard and proceeded to shout and berate the other four linemen. As the five teammates walked back to the sideline, #59 stopped and tore off his helmet. He glared at Walby then yelled, "Shut up and worry about doing your own job!"

It's almost impossible for anyone to re-create or recall an exact moment in time accurately. Everyone involved will have their own recollection of the situation. Memories fade after 25 years. "What went through your mind after the ball was snapped on that second and short during the Tiger-Cats' game in 1991?" It's an impossible question to answer.

"I don't remember exactly what I said," said Walby trying to recall the incident. "If you ask the guys, they'll all tell you I had a reputation of yapping and shooting my mouth off all the time. Nobody ever listened to me, but I can tell you, when Bauer spoke, we listened. We paid attention to him."

"As a professional athlete, you never want to show weakness or defeat or anything along those lines," said Bauer. "If your opponent knows of any weakness at all, they will take full advantage of it. They had to. It's part of their job. Hell, I did it all the time. But, on that play, we didn't do our job."

"As our center, Lyle was extremely intense," recalls quarterback Tom Burgess who played six seasons in the CFL and quarterbacked the Blue Bombers to a Grey Cup win in 1990. "He had everyone's respect and attention. He was definitely the captain of that line and he was tough as nails."

The Blue Bombers went on to win that game, 68-14 and the offensive line, considered to be the best in Blue Bomber's history, held their ground until the very last whistle.

"I was born during my father's later days of playing," said Wesley Bauer, Lyle's son. "But I will never forget watching a historical football game with my father playing on late night television. I was excited as I never had really seen any footage of my dad snapping the ball."

"I remember sitting beside him and watching that first play. He snapped the ball and the next thing I see is my dad cut block the nose tackle. I turned to my dad and said 'You were a dirty football player.' He said to me, 'In those days you had to be.'"

"My dad was one tough SOB," said Brodie Bauer, Lyle's other son. "I remember him coming home with his fingers all broken from the game the previous night. Broken fingers and all, it didn't stop him from hanging out with me, Wes, and Danni, playing games in the yard."

When asked about Bauer's toughness, Ross Hodgkinson, the Blue Bombers head athletic trainer in 1985 said, "Lyle had some ongoing knee issues prior to me starting with the team," he recalls. "At some point he was placed in a leg cast to give his one knee a chance to settle down. But Lyle, in his divine wisdom, decided one evening that he had had enough of the cast. He cut it off with a power saw in his garage. The next morning he came in, stuck his head in the training room and threw the cast at me. He said he was done with it. I was furious!"

Bauer earned the reputation throughout the league as being a smart, tough leader. "I spent 10 years battling that guy," said Mike Walker who spent eight years on the Hamilton Tiger-Cats defense and two with the Edmonton Eskimos. "We had some epic battles in those years. But he was one guy that never broke. He would never let up."

So in August 2004, when the former leader of the Blue Bomber's "Hog Line" developed a severe sore throat, he ignored it.

"I was never one to go to the doctor. I hated going to doctors," Bauer had said. "It was that don't show a weakness attitude."

But eventually he did go and after weeks of tests and appointments, he received the diagnosis: oropharyngeal cancer – stage 4. The tumour was hidden deep inside the base of his tongue.

This time it wasn't a game. The old locker room clichés of "failure is not an option" and "win at all costs" quickly became a hard reality for the former lineman. This was now life and death. There was no playbook, no business plan to reference; no teammates, coaches or trainers to lean on.

"In spite of family and friends, I had never felt so alone and unsure of what the future would bring," said Bauer. "For the first time in my life, I had no control over what was going to happen."

His first concern was his wife and children seeing him in pain. "I don't think my kids ever saw their father that vulnerable. I've always tried to be there, strength-wise," says Bauer, who has one daughter, Danni and two sons, Brodie, and Wesley.

"Once it happens, it puts you in a whole different mindset. And really, what you have to do is draw upon your past life experiences and prepare for the battle of your life. Alone."

But throughout the numerous treatments and doctors' appointments, Bauer never had a 'why me' moment.

"At the time, my thought was, 'What difference does that make when what I need to focus on is what's going to happen now?'" says Bauer.

After 42 gruelling radiation treatments, as well as chemotherapy, Bauer is now cancer-free. The radiation treatments have left him with damage to his tongue, throat, and voice box, which affect his speech, but he's grateful to be alive.

"What doesn't kill you only, makes you stronger."

That quote has been around for years. We've all seen it and heard it. It's been printed on T-shirts and embossed on coffee mugs.

Some credit the quote to the German philosopher, Friedrich Nietzsche, but he actually said it more eloquently than what we have become used to: "That which does not kill us, makes us stronger." However it's said, it turns out, he was right in Bauer's case.

There have been numerous studies and examples, medical, scientific and personal, which have shown that some survivors report positive changes and enhanced personal development after their trauma. There's even a term for it, Post Traumatic Growth or PTG. PTG is defined by any beneficial change in circumstances resulting from a major life crisis or traumatic event. People experience a positive shift by having a renewed appreciation for life or they adopt a new world view with new possibilities. They feel more personal strength, more spiritually satisfied, and their relationships improve. And some, like #59, do all that and more.

In 2005, even before he was finished with his own cancer treatments, Bauer created the Never Alone Foundation with the vision of a world where no one enters the fight against cancer feeling alone. The Never Alone Foundation is now a nationally registered charity committed to improving the lives of people affected by cancer.

When our childhood heroes face personal tragedies, they become human just like the rest of us. On the field, Lyle Bauer was a powerhouse athlete, a three time Grey Cup Champion and a member of the Blue Bombers Hall of

Fame. Off the field, he was a successful business leader and role model to many. Yet with all that going for him, he was still attacked by something completely outside of his control.

If you ask him today, he'll tell you he never wanted to fail at anything. I'm sure at some point during his battle with cancer he repeated that same line to himself he once said to Chris Walby. "Shut up and worry about doing your own job!" Bauer's job was to survive. To live another day and make someone else's path a little easier.

When we come to know our heroes through their own eyes, we understand that a hero is just an ordinary person who found the strength to persevere in spite of overwhelming obstacles. They keep moving, always, towards a goal they believed in.

Lyle now says he's more concerned with what he will leave on this Earth after he's gone than what he can take from it now.

"You can't take anything with you. That's been proven and I'm living it. But, what you can do is make sure you did something for someone else. That's really what we are supposed to do. That's our job, that's my job, and that's what people will be remembered for."

Since 2005, Lyle and the staff and volunteers of the Never Alone Foundation have raised funds to support various cancer programs and have assisted hundreds of victims and their families. But he is quick to point out that even though he started the foundation, it's not his. It never was.

His story is not complete by any means. This book is meant to tell the story of a man who works tirelessly to make the later chapters of his life far better than the earlier ones. And isn't that what life is all about.

What Doesn't Kill You

Chapter 2

Every CFL team's season has a beginning, but only one team earns the opportunity to see their season end happily. Since 1910, the Saskatchewan Roughriders have experienced the latter just four times.

The Saskatchewan Roughriders are the third-oldest professional gridiron football team in existence today. Only the Arizona Cardinals of the NFL and the CFL's Toronto Argonauts are older. The Roughriders play in the CFL's smallest Canadian market and the second-smallest major-league market in North America. Only Green Bay, Wisconsin, is smaller.

In spite of all that, the Roughriders have finished first in the CFL's Western Division seven times and have won the Western championship a record twenty-eight times. They have played in the championship game nineteen times and won four Grey Cups. The team draws loyal fans from across Saskatchewan, as well as the entire country and the iconic Green and White runs deep in Rider Nation.

Saskatoon's Lyle Bauer, born and raised right in the center of Rider Nation, had dreams of someday being able to wear the coveted Green and White.

"I grew up a Riders fan and I remember neighbours of ours having some of the Rider greats like George Reed and Wayne Shaw over during training camps in Saskatoon," said Bauer. "I was in awe of those guys and of course, I wanted to be a Rider. Who didn't? Every kid in Saskatchewan does and I was pretty determined that someday I was going to make that team."

As luck would have it Bauer was picked by the Saskatchewan Roughriders in the 5th Round of the CFL's 1979 draft. Sixty-three players were chosen that year with Bauer being picked at the thirty-eighth spot. In reality, he was a long shot.

"I wasn't a top pick, but I still felt like the King of the World when I heard the news," said Bauer. "It was pretty exciting and I worked hard that off season to get myself ready for my first CFL Training camp."

Olympic Wrestling Silver Medalist Bob Molle, also from Saskatoon, who would eventually play alongside Bauer as a Blue Bomber, recalls watching him workout in the gym. "He wasn't that big, but you could see the determination on his face. You could tell there was something special there."

In 1979, Roughriders Head Coach, Ron Lancaster was the man Bauer needed to impress during training camp. Over his 16 seasons with the Roughriders, Lancaster's team had won 170 games with him at the quarterback position and had only one losing season of 4–11–1 in 1978. That season would become Lancaster's final as the team's quarterback. He had been a player-coach for the 1977 and 1978 seasons, serving as the team's offensive co-ordinator before being appointed Head Coach.

Football training camps aren't meant to be easy. They are the ultimate proving ground. Players are pushed to their limit to demonstrate their worth. For some, it's to establish themselves into the starting lineup. For others, it's to fulfill a dream of stepping onto the field as a member of something bigger than themselves.

"As a young guy, you think you're got it all figured out," Bauer said. "But I quickly learned you really don't have a clue." Unfortunately, Bauer's first entry into professional football did not go exactly the way he had anticipated. The kid would eventually be cut by the Roughriders not once, but twice.

"They cut me as one of the last group of cuts," said Bauer. "But I did get to know the late great Ron Lancaster during my playing and managing career. He told me that it had been a very difficult decision for him to cut me. I told him all the time not to worry about it. I've got three Grey Cup Championship rings and have been to the Grey Cup eight times. I should have thanked him for cutting me."

After the last Saskatchewan cut, Bauer returned to the University of Saskatchewan where he suited up for the Huskies and continued his education.

"Heidi and I were married at that time. We both went to school and worked nights bartending to make ends meet. It was hard on us, but we always seemed to manage," said Bauer. "But I still wasn't willing to give up my dream of playing professional football."

In the fall of 1981, the University of Manitoba Bisons hosted the Saskatchewan Huskies. The Huskies lost that game but a door opened for Bauer.

"Paul Robson, the Blue Bomber's Assistant General Manager, came to see me after the game. It was just the usual chit chat but he invited me to their next camp. I knew it was a long shot and to be honest, that really was the story of my life – a long shot. I was always the young one given that I had graduated at 16. I was a little immature at times, but realized that I was going to have to really raise myself up."

"I called him a few months later to make sure he was still coming," recalls Paul Robson. "He told me he wasn't because Heidi had just started working at Safeway. I told him if he showed up, I'd find her a job in Winnipeg."

In May of 1982, Lyle and Heidi Bauer packed all their belongings into their 1979 Cougar and made their way east to Winnipeg.

In the late 70s, the Winnipeg Blue Bombers had battled and won the Grey Cup seven times since first being established in 1930. The team's last Grey Cup victories had come from a string of powerhouse seasons in 1959, 1961 and 1962.

In the early 70s, the team struggled under Coaches Jim Spavital and Bud Riley before Ray Jauch was brought in as head coach for the 1978 season. Jauch had been the Blue Bombers' running back on the team's 1961 Grey Cup win along with Hall of Fame quarterback Kenny Ploen and legendary coach, Bud Grant.

Coach Jauch inherited a team that had been 10-6 for two years, but despite the team's winning record, the Winnipeg Blue Bombers were not a team he liked. He had a reputation of being a long-range planner and would sometimes make his decisions on the basis of expected benefits down the road rather than take emergency measures to fill an immediate need.

Coach Jauch explained his philosophy in a late 80s interview with the Washington Post. "I want players with character. I tell my players they have three responsibilities; first, to some supreme being, second, to their families, and third, to the team. I tell them if they can get the first two in order, then come see me about playing football."

"I'll stick with a kid, even though a veteran might have more talent. If I think the youngster can develop in three or four years. In the long run, you're better off that way," he said in the same interview. "Look at the NFL teams that are successful; Dallas, Minnesota, Pittsburgh. The long-term planners are always the winners."

For the Winnipeg Football Club, that meant some wholesale housecleaning.

"He made a lot of changes," said former Blue Bombers' quarterback Dieter Brock in the same Washington Post interview. "When he was done there were only three or four of us left."

Chris Walby, who spent 16 years with the Winnipeg Blue Bombers recalls, "I was originally drafted by Montreal, but ended up back in Winnipeg. I only played for Coach Jauch for a one and one half seasons. He was definitely a no nonsense type of guy. He didn't know me in the beginning, but when you're 6"7 and 290, he was probably more patient with me. Maybe more than some would have been. For all he knew I was there for a cup of coffee. I remember when they converted me to play on the O-Line the next year. It was a crazy transition but Jauch and the O-Line coach, Ellis Rainsberger let me develop."

"I told Jauch, that if I was able to bring Walby in, he was going to play," said Robson. Walby became a fixture on the Blue Bombers' offensive line. During his 16 year career, he was very popular among fans and was a 9-time CFL All-Star, two time league's Most Outstanding Lineman, and three-time Grey Cup champion. He is often referred to as one of the greatest offensive linemen in the history of the CFL.

In 1979, Coach Jauch's first year, his new-look Blue Bombers finished with a record of 4-12. The next year they were 10-6 and in 1981 they finished 11-5.

Needless to say, in May of 1982 there were high hopes for the Blue and Gold's upcoming season.

"Winnipeg already had a very experienced offensive line," recalls Bauer of the 1982 training camp. "With John Bonk, Chis Walby, Nick Bastaja, Larry Butler, Bobby Thompson and others, the odds weren't in my favour going in. They had just traded for Willie Thomas and had used their territorial exemption in '81 to secure Perry Kuras, another offensive lineman. I had played with Perry at Weber State, so I knew how good he was."

An offensive lineman's role is usually limited to just a few quick steps to establish their position after the ball is snapped to the quarterback. But what follows next could be similar to a wrestling match against an opposing team's defensive player. Offensive linemen tend to be the largest players on the field, but the position still demands speed, strength, agility and balance. Most professional offensive linemen tend to be over six feet tall and weigh over 300 pounds.

On running plays, the primary job of the five offensive linemen on the line of scrimmage is to create space for the ball carrier to run, either by pushing defensive players backwards or to the side to allow the ball carrier space to run through.

On passing plays, their responsibility is to stop defensive players from tackling the quarterback before he has the chance to throw the ball. Stopping these players indefinitely is usually not possible, so the main objective of the offensive line is to slow them down, giving the quarterback the time he needs to spot an open receiver down field.

"One thing that an outsider doesn't realize at first is that the O-Line is a very unique group," said Chris Walby. "We're a tight knit group. We become like family. We play together. We battle together. We drink together. We live and die as group. Loyalty is first, talent is second. The O-Line fraternity is tight. We're brothers. We always will be."

""It got to the point where those guys had their own dialect," said Leo Ezerins. Ezerins was a linebacker for most of his CFL career, but played tight end in his 1978 rookie season with the Blue Bombers. He played for the Blue and Gold until 1982 before leaving for the Hamilton Ti-Cats. "Most of the time, when they told a joke, they were the only ones who laughed because no one else could understand what they were saying."

"If a team is built to win consistently, it is because of two things; the strengths of a stalwart defense, and a dominating offensive line," said Tom Burgess, the Blue Bombers' quarterback from 1990 to 1991. "As a quarterback, you had to have confidence in those guys up front."

"I remember Lyle coming in the locker room that first day of camp," said Walby. "He was just another chubby white kid looking for a job. We ignored him for the most part."

"To be honest, we didn't really pay much attention to any new guy that came in," said Nick Bastaja. "As a veteran, you're certainly not going to waste time getting to know them because you never know how long they'll last."

"We'd see guys like him come in all the time," said Walby. "I wasn't going to pay them any attention. Remember, if a new guy comes in, that could mean someone you're playing with, someone you already know and trust, is leaving and that's not a good feeling. Stability on the line is crucial and we'll fight to keep it."

"That first training camp was... well the first guy I saw was Bobby Thompson. 6'8" and 300 pounds," said Bauer. "It was obvious things weren't in my favour."

"It seemed like the locker room was sectioned off into three groups," recalls Bauer. "The first was for the veterans, the guys who were safe in their role with the team. The second group was for the high draft picks that would easily make the first cut. The last one was for guys like me. They should have had a sign on the wall in that section saying, "Don't unpack your shit, because you won't be around long."

"But I was determined," Bauer continued. "I'd always admired the great gifted athletes. People like James West, Tyrone Jones, Rod Hill, Michael Gray, and so many more. My motivation really didn't come from any one person. It came from chasing a lifelong dream and wanting the best for Heidi and my family."

Bauer stuck it out with pure grit and determination. "Every day for four weeks I had to battle with John Helton." Helton was a 6'3", 250 pound Canadian Hall of Fame defensive end who had played with the Blue Bombers from 1979 into the 1982 season. "He was the nicest guy ever, but that nice guy beat the hell out of me every day for four weeks."

Most football training camps are the same. Unless you're a marquee player, the others don't care where you've been or who you are. Everyone battles to secure their spot on the team roster. But members of the offensive line compete differently than an individual player. The O-Line plays as a group, a group that has to develop a tight bond to be successful. They earn respect for each other and understand their individual strengthens and weaknesses.

"I worked my ass off and my heart out during those four weeks," said Bauer. "But they released me and I was placed on the practice roster for the first game."

"That was extremely disappointing. In that short period of time I had grown to really admire the Winnipeg club. But I still wanted to play, somewhere, anywhere and I knew I could. So, I started talking to the people in Montreal and they agreed to fly me in to join their team after their first game."

But Montreal would not be in the cards for Bauer. During the Blue Bombers' first game of the 1982 season, Willie Thomas, the 225 pound starting center, blew out his knee and was done for the season.

"Paul Robson tracked me down immediately after the game and told me I was on the team. Heidi and I stayed and that was the start of my journey and the best decision I ever made."

Making the Winnipeg Blue Bombers roster was now a reality, but that was just one hurdle Bauer had cleared. With the closeness of the O-Line, he still had to be accepted by the group.

"I was now officially on the roster, but still, at that time in the CFL, there was no such thing as long term contracts. A team could release you twenty-four hours before a game and they wouldn't have to pay you. That was always hanging over me and I still felt like I was on the bubble."

One afternoon, still early in the season, Bauer entered the Blue Bombers' locker room to find his space had been completely cleared out. His locker was empty except for a note taped to the wall informing him to, "Report to Coach's office immediately and bring your playbook."

"I was furious," said Bauer recalling the incident. "It wasn't so much the idea of being cut, that had happened three times already. But in my opinion, it was a cowardly way to do it. They cleaned my stuff out and packed it all up."

"The entire locker room was dead quiet except for Lyle," said Walby. "He started screaming and punching the walls. The tension was unbelievable."

"I stormed out of that locker room straight for Coach's office," said Bauer. "That coward was going to get a piece of me."

To get to Coach Jauch's office, players had to walk down a short hallway and through the weight room. John Bonk, the veteran center was well into his workout when he spotted the agitated rookie storm into the room.

"Bonk stopped me," said Bauer." He tried to hold me back, but I wasn't going to go down easy. I was pissed."

Bauer forced his way to the doorway of the coach's office and stood solid, ready for a fight. Coach Jauch annoyed, looked up from his desk. "What the hell do want?" he asked. Bauer couldn't get a word out before the sounds of laughter burst out behind him.

"It was a prank," said Bauer. "They had set me up. I remember Walby's fat face laughing at me. I wanted to punch him so bad."

"It was hilarious," said Walby. "Bonk set it up. We had no idea what was going on. But I'll tell you, it was that moment, that prank where we knew he had not only made the team, but Lyle Bauer was now one of us."

Chapter Three

A good football team might be pleased to finish a season with an 11-5 record. A good team might be proud of the fact that they had six All-Canadian players and nine All-Division All Stars on their roster. But a great football team would never be content with any of that. The 1982 Winnipeg Blue Bombers had had a good year, but it wasn't great. #59 had a good year, but to him, it definitely wasn't great.

Despite winning eleven regular season games and beating Calgary in the West Semi Finals, the Blue Bombers lost to their Western Division rivals, the Edmonton Eskimos in the final play-off game. By beating the Blue Bombers, Edmonton advanced to the Grey Cup game and went on to win their fifth straight championship.

Bauer proudly wore the Blue and Gold for fifteen games in 1982, but he spent most of season on the sidelines in a back-up role. He saw limited action, but it was enough to make an impression with the team's management and his teammates. Still, he wasn't satisfied.

"Of course I wasn't happy to have just survived that season," said Bauer. "Yes, I was a professional football player. It was something I had been pursuing for a long time. But I was disappointed in losing that Western final and I was not happy in a back-up role. I knew I still had a lot of work to do to earn a starting position and I was prepared to do whatever it took in the off season."

He cleared out his locker during a quiet week in late November 1982. He recalls walking through the parking lot of Winnipeg Stadium. "I really don't remember feeling any insecurity about the whole situation," says Bauer. "To have insecurity, you have to be afraid of something being taken away. I was always one step away from being cut, so it was no big deal. It had happened before, but I had persevered."

"Heidi and I packed up the car and went back to Saskatoon. We both went back to working in the bars at night. I trained hard in the gym during the day and bartended in a pretty rough club. I also started studying to get my real estate license. I knew I was one step away from no football, so I had to develop something moving forward."

"I've always wanted to be stronger, faster and smarter. In '82, I didn't like that feeling of being on the bubble. As a back-up, I felt that I never really got the opportunity to prove myself."

"In the off season I needed to get stronger and I really worked at it. I always had to work on my strength. One thing I did understand was the responsibilities of the position and the playbook. Not making mistakes in those areas is crucial for the team."

Midway through the 1982 season, word was starting to spread that head coach Ray Jauch would be leaving the Winnipeg organization for the upstart Washington Federals of the United States Football League. The team had lured Jauch to be its head coach because of his success in the Canadian Football League. At the time, Ray Jauch was the fourth-winningest coach in CFL history.

"We really didn't find out he was leaving until later on in the season. I think it did have an effect on the psyche of the team in the end. It was probably hard for Ray to keep focused knowing there was a new challenge coming for him at the end of the year."

On January 25, 1983, the Winnipeg Blue Bombers introduced Cal Murphy as the team's new head coach. Murphy had been the offensive line coach with the Edmonton Eskimos under head coach Hugh Campbell. The Eskimos had won an unprecedented five straight CFL titles with star quarterbacks like Tom Wilkinson and Warren Moon. The timing was impeccable. The Eskimos had beaten the Blue Bombers 24-21 in the '82 West Division Finals just two months before the announcement.

Murphy's football credentials were impressive. In his early days he attended Vancouver College where he had been a football standout. He then moved on to play with the University of British Columbia Thunderbirds as a left-handed quarterback and defensive back as well as a brief stint with the B.C. Lions in 1956. Murphy then took over the reins at UB.C. as the Thunderbirds head coach in 1960-61. He led the team to their only undefeated season.

Following that, he became an assistant coach at Eastern Washington University under Head Coach Dave Holmes. He followed Holmes to the University of Hawaii Rainbows, and became part of the most successful coaching tenure in Hawaii history. In 1973, Murphy left Hawaii for the San Jose State Spartans to work under Head Coach Darryl Rogers.

Cal Murphy joined the CFL coaching ranks in 1974 with the B.C. Lions under Head Coach Eagle Keys, and became head coach after six games in the 1975 season. He was fired after the 1976 season and moved on to spend the 1977 season with the Montreal Alouettes under Head Coach Marv Levy.

In 1978, Murphy took a job as the offensive line coach with the Edmonton Eskimos under Head Coach Hugh Campbell and remained there until joining the Blue Bombers in 1983. His appointment was a bit of a homecoming as Murphy was born in Winnipeg in 1932. His football career seemed to have now come full circle.

"I wasn't really wasn't too concerned about a coaching change. To be honest I hoped it would give me a fresh start," said Bauer.

"Coach Jauch was always smiling and saying the right things. But you knew quickly that what he said wasn't necessarily what he was going to do. Cal, on the other hand, was an open book. You always knew where you stood and where he was coming from. That's probably why he and I got along so well. He was a 'No Bullshit' type of person."

Cal Murphy opened the 1983 Winnipeg Blue Bombers training camp with plenty of new faces looking to make an impression, but almost every player entered training camp unsure of their future. There were, after all, just 38 positions up for grabs, four of which had to be held in reserve. Nineteen spots were available to non-import players on a team's active roster and just fifteen for the imports.

"I don't think anyone knew what to think of Cal Murphy at first. But what we all found out early in camp was that it didn't matter who you were or what you had done in the past," recalls Bauer. "In his eyes, you were going to have to earn your spot on his team. He made that clear. This was his team and it was his way or you weren't going to be around."

"From day one, Cal made it obvious it was team first," said Chris Walby. "You were going to have to fight for your spot. Cal would always bring in guys to compete for your spot and that made the competition fierce. Nothing was guaranteed with that guy. There was no loyalty from Coach Cal in the beginning, but he most definitely demanded it from us."

"It didn't take long that's for sure," said Bauer who now laughs at those early days. "Cal beat the shit out of us in training camp, physically and mentally. He was the exact opposite of Ray Jauch. We hit 'til we bled and ran 'til we puked, twice a day."

"Camp Calsky" was the name given by players during that first training camp. It was a tribute to the tough hauling they had gone through. "After camp was over, we had T-shirts made that said "I Survived Camp Calsky," said Bauer.

"I had great admiration for Cal. He truly was a person where you were rewarded for what you could do and not your reputation. Work hard and you will be rewarded. Going into that camp, I was hell bent on earning a spot and contributing to the team."

By the time Murphy had finished his first Blue Bombers' training camp, the total roster turnover from the previous season was thirty-two players. Murphy was determined to build his own team.

But there was a cloud hanging over the club that didn't sit well with Murphy. Dieter Brock, the team's quarterback still hadn't reported to training camp. Brock had led the CFL in passing in 1978, 1980 and 1982 and had won back-to-back Most Outstanding Player Awards.

In 1980, Brock had signed a five-year deal with the Blue Bombers, but when Ray Jauch announced that he would be leaving for the USFL, Brock developed the urge to also head down south.

Before the start of the '83 season there had been discussions between Brock and Blue Bombers' General Manager, Paul Robson, about shortening his contract to allow him to finish his career in the USFL. But when talks fell short, Brock held out and was a no-show for camp.

"With the Dieter situation, it really didn't affect the other players," said Bauer." We understood it was the nature of the business. I knew from the outset Cal and Dieter weren't going to be a match for a variety of reasons."

"I was just fighting to get a starting job. What was going on between them was irrelevant to me. I wanted the spot on the team and I had a coach that was going to make me earn it, but I was good with that."

With the long hot days of training camp finally over, it was time to see if Cal Murphy had put the pieces together successfully. On Friday, June 10, the starting offensive line for the Blue Bombers' first exhibition game was set with Bobby Thompson and Chris Walby at the tackle position, Nick Bastaja and Lyle Bauer as guards and John Bonk at center against the Calgary Stampeders.

But without a key starting quarterback, there were still too many concerns with the offense. Murphy made the decision to dress quarterbacks Nicky Hall, Norman Gibbs, Lawrence McCullough and Brian Broomell.

"You're always a little nervous when you get to this point, mainly because of the uncertainty," Murphy told the Winnipeg Sun in an interview before the game. "But it's also a relief in a way because you come out of it with some idea of what you have to work with and how much more work needs to be done. It's a reference point."

But by the end of the evening, Murphy's excitement was over. With a 24-4 loss, the head coach discovered he had several areas of concern and the main issue was the Blue Bombers' quarterback position.

Unfortunately, the quarterback dilemma continued throughout the entire exhibition season leaving the Blue Bombers with a record of 0-4. Murphy and his team had tested the waters of the CFL's Western Division and were losers every time. The Lions, the Stampeders, the Eskimos and the Roughriders had all beaten the Blue Bombers and there was just ten day left before the league opener.

Then, suddenly, word came that Dieter Brock, may be interested in a deal to return for one final year.

Paul Robson, in a last ditch attempt, flew down to Birmingham, Alabama for a face to face, heart to heart chat with the 32-year-old quarterback and his agent, Gil Scott. Brock still had three years plus an option year left on his contract. Robson stated his position and Brock did the same. The result was...no result. Nothing had changed. Dieter Brock was not coming back to Winnipeg.

On July 2, Cal Murphy, with no other option, presented his 38 man final roster to the league office. The Blue Bombers would compete with two starting quarterbacks. Mark Jackson and Nicky Hall would share the offensive responsibilities.

Lyle Bauer's name was also on the official starting roster. Despite a slight ankle injury, Bauer would join Nick Bastaja at the guard positions. Veteran John Bonk would line up as the team's center. The tackle positions however were still in doubt. Murphy decided to use a combination of Bobbie Thompson, Frankie Smith, Derek Faggiani and Chis Walby thrown in at one spot or the other.

But in professional sports, nothing is ever as easy as it seems. Game plans and rosters can change at a moment's notice. On July 5, just three days before the season opener, Dieter Brock returned, unannounced.

Despite being a veteran quarterback with nine seasons under his belt, Brock would not dress for the opener against the Ottawa Rough Riders. Murphy stuck with his decision to use his original quarterback duo of Jackson and Hall. Dieter Brock was placed on a 14-day trial.

The result of that first game was a 26-25 loss against the Rough Riders and neither quarterback had made an impression with Murphy.

But there were positives after the first game. During training camp and the pre-season, Assistant Coach, John Gregory, had been emphasizing versatility with the team's offensive line. He knew the linemen would have to handle assignments in different positions sooner or later. It was the nature of the game.

And Gregory was right. Early in the second quarter of the Ottawa game, right tackle Chris Walby went down with an injury. Bauer was moved from his guard position to fill in for Walby, while back-up Mark Moors stepped in at the guard position. Both players executed their new positions without a mistake for the entire game.

"We learned early that Lyle had a great mind for the game," said Walby. "Not only did he know his position, but he knew exactly what others needed to be doing and when."

In week two the Blue Bombers faced their Western Division rivals, the Edmonton Eskimos. Dieter Brock had missed training camp and the entire pre-season, but the untested quarterback jogged onto the field for the third offensive series and never looked back. He led the team to a 20-18 victory.

The following weeks against Hamilton, Montreal and Toronto were all wins for the Blue Bombers. But a nagging ankle injury would sideline Bauer after the Toronto game. With the B.C. Lions next on the schedule, Murphy made the decision to leave Bauer in Winnipeg. He would utilize back-up Val Belcher at right tackle and moved the recovered Walby into Bauer's guard position on the line.

The ankle injury kept Bauer off the field for a few more days. But on September 1, just four days before the Saskatchewan Roughriders game, he was activated and back on the practice field.

Unfortunately, the team's quarterback dilemma was still not over. Dieter Brock once again walked away from the team. He was now demanding to be either traded or released. Coach Cal had no choice but to assign back-up quarterback Nicky Hall as the starter for the next game against the Roughriders.

On Saturday Sept 4, Winnipeg Blue Bombers General Manager, Paul Robson, announced that the club had suspended Dieter Brock.

On the offensive line, Mark Moors would start for Bauer. Murphy still wasn't confident that he was 100% ready and the Blue Bombers would be on the losing side of that game to Saskatchewan.

The following week, the Blue Bombers, again without Brock, would drop another one to Montreal. Next up was the Calgary Stampeders. With Bauer back on the line, the Blue Bombers left Calgary with a 19-14 win over the Stampeders.

With just over half the season over, Murphy wasn't content with the team's 6-4 record. This was his team and he was determined to make his mark.

"I remember we had two good centers at the start of training camp; John Bonk and Willie Thomas," Bauer recalls. "Cal was going to trade one of them and Calgary was interested. He told them take either one. He didn't care. They eventually took Thomas."

Murphy made it clear that he wasn't afraid to make a big deal and he showed that by eventually dealing his suspended all-star quarterback, Dieter Brock to Hamilton for veteran quarterback, Tom Clements.

At the time, thirty-year-old Tom Clements was in his eighth CFL season. He had won the Schenley Award as the CFL's top rookie in 1975 with the Ottawa Rough Riders. He remained a Rider until being traded to Saskatchewan in

1979. During that same year he was traded to Hamilton, but moved on to spend the 1980 season with the Kansas City Chiefs in the NFL. He returned to Hamilton in 1981.

Now, buoyed by the addition of a new veteran quarterback, the Blue Bombers hoped to take another step towards securing the top spot in the Western Division when Saskatchewan made another visit to the city.

Quarterback Nicky Hall would start the game because of his knowledge of Murphy's offensive system and took the Blue Bombers to a 10-7 lead mid-way through the second quarter. With 6:16 remaining, Tom Clements stepped onto the field. In his first series, Clements established control of the game. He quickly displayed his scrambling ability and talent for throwing the ball and led the team to a smashing 50-19 victory.

"We've got some sanity here for a change," Murphy was quoted as saying. "Now the players can concentrate on football."

But their new found hope wouldn't last. The following week in Hamilton against Dieter Brock and the Tiger-Cats, Clements went down on the final play of the first half. Nicky Hall stepped in to lead the team to a 34-19 victory, but Clements had suffered a fractured collarbone. The early diagnosis was that he would be out for five to six weeks and there was just four weeks left in the regular season.

Two days after the Hamilton win, the Blue Bombers announced yet another trade. Quarterback Nicky Hall, receiver Nate Johnson and defensive lineman Jason Riley were dealt to the Saskatchewan Roughriders for veteran quarterback, John Hufnagel and rookie defensive end, J.C. Pelusi.

Cal Murphy wanted an experienced quarterback and he got what he wanted.

John Hufnagel had a number of years on the field before arriving in Winnipeg. A product of Penn State, Hufnagel was a 14th round draft pick of the Denver Broncos. He first appeared in Calgary in 1976 for the final seven games of the CFL season. He started 30 games over the next two years with the Stampeders, but he eventually lost the starting role in 1979. He joined the Riders in 1980 and spent the next four years in Regina before coming to Winnipeg.

"I knew the Blue Bombers were a good football team," recalls Hufnagel. "But one thing that really stood out was they had become a very, very close knit team... especially the offensive line guys."

"At first my family was not able to join me in Winnipeg," said Hufnagel. "I ended up sharing an apartment with Val Belcher and Vernon Paul. So naturally, I did a lot of off field stuff with all the O-Line guys. I established great friendships with all of them including Lyle and his wife, Heidi."

"I really appreciated how quickly that team and especially the O-Line guys accepted me in the locker room. It was a great experience being around them. I still consider those three and half years I was a Blue Bomber to be the best times I had as a professional football player, not only for our on field accomplishments but also because of the great comradery."

"My most memorable moment of those guys occurred during a game. I had stepped back to attempt a pass and got completely annihilated by Chris Walby's man. Lyle came over to help me up and I had dirt and grass stuck in my face mask. He turned to Chris and yelled, "What are you doing? You almost got him killed!" Walby's response was "So what? He gets paid, too." All three of us just stood there in the middle of the game, laughing on the field."

But even with Hufnagel leading the offense, the next two games left the Blue Bombers empty with losses; 30-18 to the B.C. Lions and 42-23 against the Ottawa Rough Riders.

The Edmonton Eskimos would come up next at Winnipeg Stadium on October 23. No one expected a Blue Bombers' win. They were on a two game slide, riddled with injuries and on their third veteran quarterback. To make matters worse, Edmonton's quarterback, Warren Moon had been running hot and their Tom Scott – Brian Kelly receiving duo was tearing up the field and cutting holes in their opponent's defense.

But right from the opening series Hufnagel took charge. He was successful on 18 of 28 pass attempts and displayed strong leadership at the moment the Blue Bombers seemed to need it most. The Eskimos would leave Winnipeg with a 33-15 loss.

Tom Clements returned for the last regular season game against Toronto, but his return was over shadowed by a 33-9 loss to the Argonauts. The Blue Bombers would finish the 1983 season with a record of 9-7, but they still had a spot in the playoffs.

Once again the Blue Bombers road to the final had to go through Edmonton, but 1983 was not to be the Eskimos' year. The Blue Bombers, with Tom Clements, healthy and back leading the offense, would beat the Grey Cup Champion Eskimos 49-22.

Now it was on to the Western Division Final against the B.C. Lions. The sellout crowd at B.C. Place of 59,409 watched as their Lion's beat the Blue Bombers 39-21. But losing the game wasn't all the Blue Bombers lost. For the second time in the season and third of his career, quarterback Tom Clements left the game with a broken shoulder. The 1983 season was over for the Winnipeg Blue Bombers.

"During that time, the team we most respected was the B.C. Lions," said Hufnagel. "We didn't fear them, but it was a great rivalry between the two best teams in the Western Division during those years."

The team returned to Winnipeg the following day to clean out their lockers. It was a sad end to the 1983 season, but it wasn't all doom and gloom.

"Despite that loss, we were still a good team," recalls Bauer. "We were a good team with a real sense that greatness was just around the corner."

"That season was a time that we knew as a group, we could have something special. Cal was tough, but he was fair. He didn't care who you were, he wanted to know what you could do for his team. There was a sense amongst the lineman and others that we could create something special if we stuck together. The brotherhood grew closer and it continues to this day."

"They were considered an excellent O-Line because of their overall size, experience and athleticism," said Hufnagel. "Walby, Bauer, Bonk, Bastaja, Molle, Belcher, Moors, formed an intimidating group. Because of those guys, the Blue Bombers always had a strong running game due to their ability to move the line of scrimmage."

"Lyle was a very intelligent player," Hufnagel continued. "When I first joined the team, he mostly played guard but would line-up as a center on occasion. Because of his high football IQ, he was able to be moved around and play at a high level. He was a good student of the game and fully prepared himself both mentally and physically every week. He was very well respected by his teammates because of his consistent effort."

"During my first season, I was always on pins and needles knowing that, as a back-up, I could be the first in line to go," said Bauer. "Now I had a starting job on a very good football team. I had to keep getting better."

"I did miss some time that season with a bad ankle. For several games I played with a TENS unit strapped to my leg. A TENS unit sends electrical impulses to disrupt the pain. I would have it on and turn it up as the game went on. Sometimes I had to come out after a game on crutches because I couldn't walk. I did that for at least six games. But that ankle would nag me for the rest of my career."

"When you're in that situation with an injury, there wasn't someone patting you on the back, assuring you everything was going to be okay. It doesn't work that way in football. It's about being a good soldier and getting the job done, regardless of personal risk. It was and has to always be about the team and doing whatever you can until you can't do it anymore."

"I know I got some of that from Cal. He demanded loyalty and he was very loyal to people who were loyal to him. He made us understand that loyalty and respect had to be earned and once you had it, you could never breach it."

"Without question, Cal Murphy was the most influential person in my life. I learned from him, good and bad. We didn't always see eye to eye and sometimes we fought like hell. But he was special."

"Because of those years, I am loyal to a fault. I know it, but it is very important to me. It has to do with believing in someone and knowing they can and will get the job done."

"Too many people are too quick to make a knee jerk reaction when they're in a difficult situation. Don't get me wrong, if I believe a person has gotten to the point where they no longer can do the job and can't take an organization to the next step, then changes have to be made. I have no problem making difficult decisions when they are necessary."

"It's was about loyalty; loyalty to a cause, to that brotherhood that was starting to come together. And realizing that it is all bigger than you. Those were different times and different mentalities, but proven results. And when I think about it today, I wouldn't change a thing."

Chapter Four

In late April of 1984, when no one was really thinking about football, the Winnipeg Blue Bombers signed Lyle Bauer to a long term contract.

"When players don't have a contract, the contract becomes the topic of all of their conversations and not football," Cal Murphy was quoted as saying in the Winnipeg Free Press. "Being without a contract is distracting for these guys."

"Heidi and I had bought our first home in Crestview," said Bauer recalling that first contract signing. "It was a great feeling to know that the club was prepared to give me some security. In the off season I was busy training, building my real estate career and spending time with my family. I think we just felt a little more secure even though we still knew it could end at any time."

"I don't recall the exact amount of the contract," said Bauer. "But I do know I never made over $80,000 a year playing football."

Now this was 1984, but to put things in perspective, Trent Williams, a seven year veteran, left tackle with the Washington Redskins signed a 5 year, $68,000,000 contract in 2015. His contract included an $8,500,000 signing bonus, $41,250,000 guaranteed, and an average annual salary of $13,600,000. Williams' one year salary in 2017 was almost enough to cover the salaries of every CFL player in the league in 1984.

"For me, it was good to know there was some security and commitment with a contract," said Bauer. "But you have to understand, back then, no contracts were ever guaranteed. They could still cut me at any time."

The Winnipeg Blue Bombers opened their 1984 training camp on May 19 with 79 players on a soggy field at St. James Collegiate. Cal Murphy had a theme for that year's gruelling two-a-day workouts. In the off season, Murphy and his coaching team were concerned about getting caught short at any position. Depth was a concern, so they had most of the players focus on strength and position flexibility.

"1984 was different in that we weren't getting used to a new coach," recalls Bauer. "The systems were already in place. We just had to improve in some talent areas and implement those strategies flawlessly."

With the '83 Western Final loss still lingering, Murphy stepped in and executed his plan on day one. For the offensive line, Val Belcher was shuffled to left guard leaving Bauer at left tackle.

The two tackles play outside of the guards on the line. Their role is primarily to block on both running and passing plays. For right-handed quarterbacks like Tom Clements and John Hufnagel, the left tackle is charged with protecting the quarterback from being hit from behind, known as his "blind side." Because of that responsibility, the left tackle is usually the most skilled player on the offensive line. Players put in that position are typically taller than interior offensive linemen because they need to keep a clear separation from defensive linemen in both pass and run blocking situations. As well, they tend to have quick footwork skills as they often engage for longer periods against containing or rushing defensive ends.

"Now, I was no Chris Walby by any means," said Bauer. "But being asked to play the blindside tackle means the coaching staff has confidence in you. It's a huge responsibility."

"Cal wanted to go with an all Canadian O-Line and he felt that my knowledge of the playbook and my diversity would give him that option," said Bauer. "The change would allow him to employ another import starter on defense which set the stage for one of the most dominating defenses in the league for years to come. "

During training camp the offensive line was being juggled so the coaching staff could gauge Bauer's performance as a tackle. Bobby Thompson, Val Belcher and Pieter VandenBos were all getting a look at Bauer's former guard position.

Most of Murphy and offensive line coach Gregory's drills were more technique oriented as opposed to the usual individual contact. They focused on the concept of team rather than the play of an individual player.

But that's not to say the '84 Training Camp was any less intense than the previous year.

"Most veterans usually start out slower because after you've played a few years, you begin to realize you have to pace yourself. You want to gradually peak at the proper time without burning yourself out," said Bauer. "But that year I had to throw all that aside and show the coaches what I could do right from the start."

On June 3 the starting line-up for the first exhibition game was finalized. The Blue Bombers would start Bauer at left tackle, Val Belcher at left guard, John Bonk at center, Mark Moors at right guard and Chris Walby at right tackle against the Saskatchewan Roughriders. Bastaja was left in Winnipeg due to an injury.

Early in the game, Bauer struggled in his new position. "Things were a little tough for me early in that game. I was playing against a pretty good guy in Willie Jones." Jones was a nasty 6' 5", 260 pound beast who had once been drafted by the Los Angeles Raiders in the second round of the NFL draft. He had joined the Roughriders that year and was determined to make an impact to earn a spot for himself.

"My footwork was coming along, but I had to get used to the idea that I was no longer working in an enclosed area. At tackle, they've got all that space out there for your opponent to get around you. I did manage to settle down as the game went on."

Football coaches don't place much emphasis on pre-season statistics. They mix and match their line-ups in order to get a read on as many players and situations as possible. But Murphy did say that Bauer did an admirable job in that first game after he settled in.

In the pre-season, the team would go 3-1, beating Saskatchewan, Calgary and Edmonton. The last pre-season game brought a 13-4 loss against the B.C. Lions.

When the final 1984 starting roster was handed into the league office, the Winnipeg Blue Bombers were going to compete with Cal Murphy's all Canadian line. Lyle Bauer would lineup at left tackle, Nick Bastaja at left guard, John Bonk at center, Mark Moors at right guard and Chris Walby at right tackle. Val Belcher was a utility lineman while Richard Nemeth and Pieter VandenBos had been placed on the reserved list.

One of the hardest cuts to affect the team was to import tackle, Bobby Thompson.

"Bobby Thompson became a victim of the numbers game," Cal Murphy was quoted as saying to the Winnipeg Sun. "With Dieter Brock, you could have those big linemen in there because Dieter was a pure drop-back passer. Now we have a little more mobility at quarterback and can get away with a bit smaller linemen." Thompson had reported to camp weighing in at 325 pounds, which didn't help his mobility.

Bobby Thompson was part of a line that featured John Bonk, Butch Norman and Larry Butler. The "Big Cat" played with the Blue Bombers from 1979 to 1984 and was a key figure in the group that helped Dieter Brock win back-to-back CFL Most Outstanding Player Awards in 1980 and 1981. Thompson was also one of the more popular members of the Winnipeg Blue Bombers, both with players and the fans. He was known as a gentle giant of a man who got along with everybody.

"Bobby was definitely a casualty of the all Canadian line. "Big Cat" as we called him, was a great guy and monster of a man," recalls Bauer.

After leaving the Blue Bombers, Thompson went on to play six games with the Hamilton Tiger-Cats for the balance of the 1984 season. He would return to Winnipeg after his marriage ended and occasionally work as a security guard or bouncer at various hotels around the city.

"His life did go downhill for a while," recalls Bauer. "But he did get his shit together later in life. During my time in management, I met several times with Bobby and helped him out financially and otherwise on a personal basis."

In late January 2005, at 46 years old, Bobby Thompson died of a massive heart attack in the lobby of his St James apartment building. Some sources had stated his weight had ballooned to almost 500 pounds and the former lineman spent all of his time alone and away from public life.

"He always tried to give back through amateur football and I would like to think, in some small way, I helped him get back on track. He always thanked me for that. These are things I have never talked about with anyone. Not even my wife. We lost a great guy far too early."

The result from game one for the new look Winnipeg Blue Bombers could only be described as dismal. The final score of 24-17 didn't come close to telling the full story. The Calgary Stampeders didn't win so much as the Blue Bombers gave the game away with 15 unnecessary turnovers.

But, this was 1984 and this was a good team on the cusp of being great. By September 30, the Winnipeg Blue Bombers would be in 1st place in the West Division with an impressive 9-3-1 record.

"Not only were we good back then, but that team was close," recalls Willard Reaves, the Blue Bombers all star running back. "There was definitely a close brotherhood amongst the guys."

With four games left in the regular season, the Blue Bombers would head east to face the Toronto Argonauts.

The previous meeting between the two teams resulted in a close 28-26 victory for the Winnipeg club.

But this outing would be different. The team would suffer two losses; one on the scoreboard and another on the offensive line. Bauer had strained his knee ligaments and suffered cartilage damage in the 31-19 loss in Toronto.

"The turf was brutal, like hard concrete. The Blue Jays had played there the night before and there was a seam in the turf from the outfield fence. It had been badly covered up and when I was running down the field, I caught it and my knee buckled. I stayed in play, but I knew something was really wrong."

"We got back to Winnipeg and I got an MRI. The result showed a torn anterior cruciate ligament. We iced it and rehabbed for a few days and then they thought we would try it."

"I remember going out knowing it was a bad idea, but I was a good soldier."

"I had to do some one on ones with James Wolfe to test it out. The first one wasn't bad. The second one not as good, but then during the third one, my knee gave out completely. The pain was brutal. I had to be carried off the field. "

"The medical diagnosis was that I had damaged my medial meniscus and completely severed my anterior cruciate. Surgery came after to clean up the meniscus, but I never did have my ACL repaired and still haven't. I've just lived with it."

With Bauer out at least until the final game of the season, the team originally announced that Val Belcher would take Bauer's spot on the line.

But Murphy changed his mind at the last minute. Val Belcher was an import and in order to keep his all Canadian line and the import/non import ratio, he needed that position filled by a Canadian. Enter Richard Nemeth.

"Richard was a young kid with lots of talent and ultimately started there at the position. Cal decided to go with inexperience at the position so he could keep his defense intact."

October 8 against Calgary was a Blue Bomber 46-8 win followed by a 30-11, win against Edmonton on October 13.

But despite the wins, there was a great deal of pressure put on the rookie Richard Nemeth. Chris Walby admitted the line felt Bauer's absence. "He was certainly a missed factor. He was having a really good year and was playing superb football up until his injury," said Walby in the Winnipeg Sun.

"I tried working out before the Lion's game," said Bauer. "But it just wasn't good. I really wanted to get in badly, but if I couldn't contribute my all to the team, I had to face reality."

"He'll be back," said Walby. "He'll definitely be missed, but I guess he'll have to wait until next year."

Without Bauer, the Blue Bombers would leave B.C. Place with a 20-3 loss. But the team was still 11-4-1 for the season and sitting in 2nd place in the Western Division.

Bauer would go on to miss the 55-20 Semi-Final win against the Edmonton Eskimos and the 31-14 Western Final win against the B.C. Lions.

In the east, the Hamilton Tiger-Cats took on the Montreal Concordes in the Eastern Semi-Final, beating them, 17-11. The following week, the Tiger-Cats walked away with a tight 14-13 victory against the Toronto Argonauts and the 1984 Grey Cup clash was set. On November 18, at Edmonton's Commonwealth Stadium., the Winnipeg Blue Bombers would face the Hamilton Tiger-Cats.

Before the game, most of the experts believed this was a mismatch on paper, and they turned out to be correct. But not before the Hamilton Tiger-Cats took an early 14-3 first quarter lead. The Blue Bomber's quarterback, Tom Clements was ineffective in the opening 15 minutes, getting picked off two times. Both interceptions led to Hamilton scores. Tiger-Cats quarterback, Dieter Brock, scored on a 15-yard scamper and completed a seven-yard pass for the other major.

But the Blue Bombers would not go down without a fight. Eventually they would dominate and take over control of the game. The Blue Bombers got their initial points on a 25-yard field goal by Trevor Kennerd to close out the opening quarter, then went on to score 27 points in the second quarter.

Tom Clements improved as the game wore on, completing a 12-yard touchdown pass to Joe Poplawski to put Winnipeg in the lead for good.

The turning point in the game came at 2:26, just before halftime when Dieter Brock was levelled by Winnipeg linebacker, Tyrone Jones. The ball was knocked loose and nose tackle Stan Mikawos picked up the loose ball and ran 22 yards for a touchdown. This put the Blue Bombers in front 24-17.

Willard Reaves, the CFL Most Outstanding Player, scored a pair of touchdowns on three-yard runs. His action was limited due to an injured shoulder, but he did rush for 64 yards in the game.

Blue Bombers' cornerback David Shaw intercepted a Dieter Brock pass in the second quarter and returned the ball 26 yards to the Hamilton 28 to help set up one of Reaves' scores.

"Willard was amazing all season," said Bauer. "As a lineman, you wanted to open a hole for him out of fear he would run you over if you didn't. He was probably one of the most powerful running backs I ever played with."

Clements had been playing the entire game with a rib injury, but despite his control of the game, a decision to make a change came from the sideline. Blue Bombers' back-up quarterback John Hufnagel stepped in and completed a four-yard touchdown pass in the fourth quarter to complete the victory.

The Blue Bombers had scored 44 unanswered points, completely shutting out the Tiger-Cats in the final 30 minutes. But it was without their starting left tackle who was forced to watch the game away from his team.

"Missing that Grey Cup was one of the worst feelings I've ever had," said Bauer. "The team took the injured players to the Grey Cup and tried their best to involve us, but we weren't part of it. That was hard to swallow."

"That was the same year that Dan Huclack broke his leg so he and I hung out together. On game day we ended up going with all of the wives which, in itself, was kind of humiliating. Cal wouldn't allow injured players on the sidelines, but we did get to the locker room to partake in the victory celebration."

"Going to the Grey Cup Game as a player is supposed to be difficult. But sitting out was is even tougher. I understand it has to be team first and that was a hard lesson. I was even more determined after that to make sure there would be more to come."

Chapter Five

It wasn't luck that placed the Grey Cup in the hands of the 1984 Winnipeg Blue Bombers. It was the result of months, if not years of each individual's hard work and dedication, team-building and constant preparation.

"Not being on the field with the guys in '84 stung," said Bauer. "The pain of missing that moment would last longer than the pain I felt from the injury. I was determined to never let that happen again. I was going to come back stronger than ever, physically and mentally."

Bauer spent the '84 off season working on strengthening his right knee, dealing with a growing family and building his real estate business. "For me an off season was never really off," he said.

"He never stopped," said Chris Walby. "That guy always had something on the go. He was always working on a deal or having something to close."

Coming off one of the best seasons in the history of the franchise, and with Grey Cup fever still in the air, the Blue Bombers opened their 1985 training camp on a high. Thirty-nine veterans reported for their first full workouts at the Velodrome in late May.

It was well known in the locker room and around the CFL that the Blue Bombers' offensive line had developed into one of the best in the league. On day one, Bauer was listed as the starting left tackle and he had experience in the guard slot as well.

"I wasn't too concerned about which position I would play. I had experience at both tackle and guard."

Unless there was an injury or other unforeseen circumstance, the other starters on the offensive line with Bauer would be John Bonk at center, Walby as the other tackle, and Bastaja and Moors at guards. Nemeth would be back-up tackle and guard.

In the previous season, the team had ordered all their offensive linemen to strap on knee braces. "I called mine the Cadillac," said Bauer. It was a Lennox-Hill brace that cost around $700 he recalls. The other linemen went with a much lighter brace.

There was still minor fluid buildup in Bauer's damaged knee, but his recovery was on schedule and holding up. But as usual, that didn't stop Cal Murphy from bringing in a few new bodies to stir things up and keep everything competitive. Enter Pat Langdon, Paul Palma and David Black.

"Those grueling two-a-day workouts seem to creep up on you. You're just never prepared for a Cal Murphy training camp," said Bauer. "One minute I'm in dress pants and a tie hosting an Open House and the next, I'm getting my ass kicked by a 250 pound guy who thinks he can take my job."

One of the new bodies was Paul Palma. Palma was in his third season in the CFL and had once started on the offensive line for the Hamilton Tiger-Cats. He was acquired from the Tiger-Cats in late '84 and played briefly in the 1984 Grey Cup game for Winnipeg.

"Paul was a great guy that was secured as a back-up," said Bauer. "Pat Langdon, on the other hand was a high draft pick that had all of the talent in the world, but for some reason, he just didn't have what it took to play and get the job done. He didn't progress in the manner needed to be a consistent starter."

In the off season, Joe Mack, the Blue Bombers' Player Personnel Director, had scouted a young kid named David Black. Black was a 23 year old from Wilfrid Laurier University in Waterloo with tight end experience. In the beginning he was considered small for an offensive lineman. Reporting to camp at just 230 pounds meant he was going to have a tough time breaking into the ranks. And he needed work.

Murphy and offensive line coach, Gregory, did some shuffling to get a good look at their entire crew during the preseason. Depth was once again the priority and they knew they were starting to develop it. After four preseason games, the Blue Bombers' preseason record would even out at 2-2.

"Those guys were tight," said Black, recalling his first look at Bauer and the other offensive line veterans. "Their knowledge and intensity was second to none. I knew it was going to be hard to crack that lineup, but I was pretty determined to make it."

"Blackie fit in right away," said Walby. "The coaches knew he needed work, but we all could tell there was something there."

"Blackie just had something extra," recalls Bauer. "Tenacity, talent, and he really fit in with the rest of us."

Murphy continued shuffling members of the offensive line at the start of the regular season. The combination of veterans, rookies and back-ups continued to dominate in the league. The entire Blue Bombers' offense was racking up impressive numbers while their defense was the cause of nightmares for their opponents. The 1985 Winnipeg Blue Bombers were 7-2 at the beginning of September.

But in the '80s, the balance of power in the CFL could be fickle and prone to change by a sprained knee, a broken collarbone or a torn muscle. The line that separates a good team from a truly great team is much more defined than it might seem to people outside the locker room. And Cal Murphy still expected more.

On September 4, linebacker James "Wild" West was released from the St. Louis Cardinals. West had been a key member of the Calgary Stampeders defense from 1982 to

1984, and had tested the waters of the NFL after becoming a free agent in the CFL.

According to some media reports, several CFL teams had expressed an interest in acquiring West.

"Yeah, I did have a few inquiries. There was interest," said West. "And, yes, the Bombers were trying to convince me. But to be honest, I didn't need convincing. There was no way I was going to come back to the CFL and have to face Bauer, Walby and that group two or three times a year."

"My style of play was to play side to side until I saw a break in the line," said West known for his tenacity at chasing down quarterbacks. "The only way I could ever get around guys like Bauer and Walby was to hope they hit the ground first. I was quick enough to get around them because they couldn't get up fast," he laughed.

"But I really hated playing against them. They were so good," recalls West. "Can't beat 'em, then join 'em," he said.

"I was nervous walking in there for the first time. I remember once playing against them. I knocked out Joe Poplawski. But you know, the first thing Joe did when he saw me walk into the locker room was give me a hug," laughs West. "I guess he was glad I was playing for them now and not against them, too."

"I don't remember who said it, but on day one I was told, "You may have been all that in Calgary, but you're in Winnipeg now and you are not all that, you're all this," said West. In other words, James 'Wild' West was told to leave his ego at the door.

"One of the first things that first hit me was that this was a very close group. The O-Line guys and the linebackers had a special relationship. It was definitely a brotherhood."

By mid-September, the Blue Bombers would activate West into the line-up replacing Gary Moten who was left behind as punishment for missing a team practice. It was a short week of preparation and Murphy felt none of his players could afford to miss a practice with the Saskatchewan Roughriders coming in.

"Man, I wanted to play with Tyrone Jones," said West. "I was excited. I knew Ty and I would work well together. We played a similar style."

With West in the line-up, and a healthy squad, the Blue Bombers went on to beat the Roughriders 49-3.

But the following week in Toronto, the Blue Bombers would lose a close one to the Argonauts, 27-24.

Back in Winnipeg the following day, Head Coach, Cal Murphy admitted himself to the cardiac unit of the Health Sciences Centre with a mild heart attack. Murphy had previously suffered a severe heart attack in 1979 while with the Eskimos. No one realized that this would be just the beginning of Murphy's heart issues.

So, with the Bombers heading into two key Western Division, back to back games against the B.C. Lions, line-backing coach, Fred Glick, was named acting head coach.

In the first game, sometime in the second quarter, a Blue Bomber offensive lineman would fall on Bauer's leg while he battled with an opponent. He went down on the field and immediately knew something was wrong. After a hard fought training camp in an effort to regain his starting position and helping the team get to a 10-3 record, Bauer's reward would be another knee injury.

"When we got back to Winnipeg the diagnosis wasn't good," said Bauer. "Strained knee ligaments in the other knee." For the second consecutive season, #59 would miss the last month.

The Winnipeg Blue Bombers ended the 1985 season with a record of 12 wins and 4 losses, finishing second in the CFL's West Division. They were set to play in their 4th Western Division Final in five years, but unfortunately they succumbed to the first place B.C. Lions in the final, 42-22.

So ended the Winnipeg Blue Bombers one-year reign as Grey Cup Champions.

"Again, we had a very good football team in '85 and were in contention from day one. But the beauty of the '83, '84 and '85 seasons were the epic battles and the rivalry between us and the B.C. Lions," said Bauer. "That '85 Western Final should have been the Grey Cup. It was the two best teams in the league and the rivalry between us was one of the most intense times for most of our careers."

"Yes, I was injured again and it was extremely frustrating. But, I wasn't done. I was far from out."

Chapter Six

When the Winnipeg Blue Bombers opened their 1986 training camp, Head Coach Cal Murphy had 90 players ready to battle for 38 spots on the team's roster. There were hopeful rookies and draft picks looking to make an impact, and a handful of well-known veterans focused on continuing to move from good to great.

For the second straight season, 1986 was being considered as Lyle Bauer's comeback. Two knee injuries had sidelined him for three of the team's most important games in the last two years. The first, forced him to miss the '84 Western Final and the Grey Cup game. The '85 injury forced him to sit out the Western Final against their rivals, the B.C. Lions.

"Both knee injuries were flukes; getting caught in a seam and then having someone fall on me," said Bauer. "I worked awfully damn hard on my legs that off season. I was doing a lot of weight training and playing squash. At the end of that '85 season I said I wasn't done, and I meant it."

"In '86 I checked in at around 255 pounds," recalls Bauer. "I had lost 15 pounds from the previous year and felt stronger and even more determined to go all 18 games."

The first day of camp was a tough one. He wondered if his right knee would handle the strain after the last injury. "The first little bit went slow. When I first lined up and went into my stance, I wondered whether it would hold out," he said. "It did and after that things kept getting better."

The day a player steps on the field, he has to become a warrior, a gladiator for the rest of the season. On the first day there has to be no question that he will be prepared to work every day. But every year there's someone new coming in who wants that job. Everyone wants to be a starter, but the competition only makes a player better.

"There were always new bodies coming into camp," said Chris Walby. "But we never really paid attention to any of them. If they made the team, maybe we might talk to them, but otherwise there was no need to get to know them."

Football training camps are often chaotic and more often than not, violent. When the hitting starts, tempers flare. Two times a day the offensive and defensive lines pound each other to the ground. After a few days, it's like waiting for a twig to snap. There's going to be fights, no doubt about it.

"I'll admit, I went at it a few times. There was Vernon Pahl and John Sturdivant. I don't remember why, it just happens," said Bauer.

"Lyle was one tough son of a bitch," said Chris Walby. "I remember the one year Leon Hatziioannou came in. He was a huge defensive lineman we had just picked up from Hamilton and he was going to try to make the team. We had a game the next day so practice is supposed to be toned down a bit. You don't go frickin' nuts. You take it easy."

"Well, not Leon. Hatzie goes nuts. It's almost like he was saying, 'Watch me Coach. Watch what I can do,' and he just goes off. Well, Lyle does this big spin, flies at him, and forearms him across the side of the knee. Hatzie never did that again."

There is a bond that's forced to be created by the adversity players endure in training camp. The intensity and pressure of the situation can make or break a player. "Even if you get into a fight on the field, you better go into the lunch room or the team meeting and say "No hard feelings. It's the job," said Bauer. "Out there, it's hit or be hit; win at all costs."

In professional football, few units are tighter-knit than the offensive line. In the previous year, new comer David Black had been rotated in and out of the lineup with Bauer, John Bonk, Mark Moors and Chris Walby. "All through '85, we knew we were getting into something special," said David Black.

"Yeah, back then, we tore it up, man," said Chris Walby. "We were all brothers through and through, on and off the field. Lyle and I were roomies on the road for 10 years."

"I remember those days," said Bauer's wife, Heidi. "The team becomes your family. We would celebrate the holidays together. There was always a special closeness."

"As you can imagine, growing up with a Winnipeg Blue Bomber as your dad was any kids dream," said Brodie, Bauer's son. "Free season tickets every year and unlimited access to the facility during the season as well as amazing seats to any concert events at the stadium were just some of the perks."

"It was always easy to make friends at school," Brodie continued. "I was a rather shy kid, however as soon as the other kids found out who my Dad was, it was as though all the sudden everybody wanted to be my friend. I kind of laugh thinking about it now. If it wasn't for my Dad I probably would of grown up that quiet introverted kid with a few close friends. But because of my Dad and his larger than life, omnipresent influence on the city of Winnipeg, everybody knew who I was and I became a lot more extroverted than I would have ever imagined. I believe his life as a Blue Bomber had a profoundly positive effect on my life growing up."

There's nothing that reveals the true story of a successful football team more accurately than the depth chart. And there's also nothing that changes more quickly. On the first day of 1986 training camp, the Blue Bombers offensive line suffered a serious blow. On the advice of the team's physicians, John Bonk was being forced to retire. Nerve problems in his neck and shoulder from a late season game in Montreal had not healed properly and the recommendation was that Bonk retire from professional football.

John Bonk's pro-football career began when the Hamilton Tiger-Cats invited him to training camp in 1972. In his first season, his play was mostly with their developmental team, but in '73, he played every game at linebacker position until he was traded to Winnipeg in October of that year.

Bonk originally started at the linebacker position in Winnipeg, but was quickly switched to center, the position he played for the rest of his career. To his credit, Bonk had not missed a regular season game between 1973 and 1985. He finished career with 202 games as a key member of the Winnipeg Blue Bomber.

"J.B. did have neck issues in the previous year," said Bauer. "I didn't think the doctors were going to pass him on his physical."

There was another factor that could possibly have had an influence in Bonk's forced retirement. "He was also making good money and I'm sure that was a factor. Cal and J.B. didn't have the best relationship, as they had butted heads over money before."

"That decision was tough on us as a group," said Bauer. "We were very, very close. It kind of brought the whole offensive line down a little bit. J.B. was one of the best centers to ever play the game and his absence could have been a big hit for the team."

As well as cleanly snapping the ball to the quarterback, the center's responsibility is to recognize what the other team's defensive line is trying to do and to communicate that information to the rest of the linemen.

Cal Murphy announced in the pre-season that Mark Moors would fill Bonk's role at center, but that didn't happen. "Mark was primarily a back-up," said Bauer. "He was undersized and struggled in one on ones. He was always a gamer and gave it his all on every play and he was the best long snapper we had."

"Mike Hameluck took the center position for a while, but he struggled with making the calls on the line," he continued. "So, at some point, Cal had me making the line calls from the right guard spot which was difficult, but it worked for a while. That's what led me to being the starting center the following year."

In the off season, the Blue Bombers had drafted Saskatoon native Bob Molle in the 9th round. At 6'4" and 275 lb., Molle had joined both the wrestling team and the football team while attending Simon Fraser University and quickly became a standout in both sports. In 1984 he had won a Silver Medal for Canada as a Super Heavyweight wrestler at the Los Angeles Olympics.

"I remember watching Lyle in Saskatoon," said Molle. "I was younger and would watch him working out at the gym."

"Bob Molle came in as a defensive lineman and started some games when Stan Mikawos was hurt," recalls Bauer. "He really wasn't suited to that position, but he was a good athlete, so he was moved to O-Line the next year. You could tell Bob was just going to get the job done and be successful. That's his mentality."

Cal Murphy set his offensive line prior to the opening regular season game against the defending Grey Cup champion, B.C. Lions. Bauer would line up with Nick Bastaja, David Black, Chris Walby, Mark Moors, Bob Molle, Mike Hameluck and Richard Nemeth.

"We had a great crew," said Walby. "We all knew that if I'm in there or one of the other guys was in, the job was going to get done."

"I used to call them my White Horses," said Willard Reaves. "I owe a lot to those guys. They were the best in the league."

By mid-September, the team was 7-5 going into Toronto to face the Argonauts. "I remember Cal and I made each other a deal before that Toronto game," recalls Bauer. It was the one year anniversary of Bauer's left knee injury and Murphy's second heart attack. "The deal was that both of us would come back to Winnipeg healthy."

"Cal and I had a special relationship," Bauer recalls. "I don't remember exactly when that started, but it was probably around that time. He started counting on me more and more to get things done. He knew I would do whatever was needed and whatever he asked."

"We used to bug Lyle all the time," said Walby. "When we were on the road, Lyle was the only one who had an open pass to Cal's room. After a game Lyle would say 'Let's go for a beer,' but instead of hitting a bar, we'd go to Cal's room. I was an older veteran so I don't think Cal gave a shit. But I don't think I should have been privy to some of their discussions."

"Cal would have a couple of sodas and the two of them would talk," said Walby. "He would talk about who they were going to cut and who should start where. I would just sit there laughing my ass off just hoping they wouldn't say my name."

"Cal knew my work ethic," said Bauer. "Having a full time job in the off-season and playing was tough, but I did it. Besides Heidi, Cal Murphy probably had the most influence in me becoming the person I am today."

The Winnipeg Blue Bombers would finish the 1986 season in third place in the West Division with a record of 11-7. Their post season record was 0-1, once again losing to the B.C. Lions, 21-14.

Many said the '86 season had ended with too many questions left unanswered.   Willard Reaves and Joe Poplawski were contemplating retirement. There were option year players like Sean Kehoe, Ken Hailey and John Hufnagel whose futures weighed heavily on the team. Quarterback Tom Clements' injured shoulder was still an issue and he was looking forward to a future career in law.

"As usual, that West Division was extremely competitive," said Bauer. "Third place was tough and even tougher losing to B.C. in the Western Semi Final again. We all felt that there were things that needed to be done to improve our club and we knew they would have to start early in the off season."

And they did. During the first week of January 1987, Blue Bombers' General Manager, Paul Robson, announced his intent to leave to take over the GM responsibilities for the Ottawa Rough Riders. Coach Cal Murphy would step up as the Blue Bombers' new GM.

One of Robson's first announcements was the appointment of Fred Glick as the new Ottawa head coach. Glick, the Blue Bombers' defensive coordinator, had filled in for Murphy after he had suffered his heart attack.

Then in early February, quarterback John Hufnagel joined the Saskatchewan Roughriders as an assistant coach.

Overall, the entire CFL was not in good financial shape. In the '86 season, the Blue Bombers had lost $586,000, the Edmonton Eskimos lost $1.1 million, the Saskatchewan Roughriders lost more than $2 million and the Montreal Alouettes lost more than $4 million. The Ottawa Rough Riders were sold for $1 after the previous owner had declared a $5 million dollar loss during the five years he had owned the team.

At the end of February, the Winnipeg Blue Bombers joined four other CFL teams in asking their players to take pay cuts. "We were all asked to take pay cuts," said Bauer. "I knew I wasn't making the most and I told Cal my number stays or I am done. From talking to a few of the other guys, I knew Cal had already done some "special arrangements" with other players to make it look like a pay cut, but really it wasn't."

"I had fought very hard to make it to the CFL. In the past I had signed minimum contracts for the sake of the team. I played multiple positions for the team, played when hurt for the team and played when I shouldn't have played, all for the sake of the team. After five years I felt I had reached a level that I didn't feel that I was overpaid, but it was still acceptable to me. I wasn't going back salary wise. There was principle behind that for me and I had to stand my ground."

"I had a young family to provide for and with me, that is a line that I won't cross. It could have been to my detriment, but I could live with that."

On March 4, in a surprise move, the Winnipeg Blue Bombers introduced Mike Riley as their new head coach. Riley had been the Bomber's secondary coach for the '83-'85 seasons before moving on to become the defensive coordinator at Northern Colorado University.

While most were looking for Cal to appoint a seasoned CFL veteran coach, Riley, at 33 years-old, would be the league's youngest coach. Riley was also the son of Bud Riley, who had served as the Blue Bombers' head coach from 1974-77.

"Mike had this way about him that you just wanted to help him succeed," said Bauer. "He was sincere, thoughtful, and just a good man."

"He was also a brilliant football man and he didn't motivate with fear. He motivated with knowledge, sound schemes and innovation. Cal was brilliant as well, but as we all knew, Cal projected a gruff exterior. My youngest son loved Cal, but he always called him the 'Grouch.' That was his nickname in our family."

"Mike was a defensive guru and Cal, offensive; a dynamic pair. They were two very different guys, but at the core, very similar. They both loved to win and despised losing."

73 players reported to Coach Riley's first Blue Bombers' training camp in the last week of May. But three key personnel from the previous season, Willard Reaves, James Murphy and Joe Poplawski had yet to report due to unresolved contract issues.

Willard Reaves had been one of the players targeted on the Blue Bombers for a potential salary cut. At the time, the 27 year-old Reaves was the highest paid running back in the league. The four year veteran had a contract worth $150,000 per season with two years remaining.

Wide receiver, James Murphy was targeted as well, but he was one of the first of the three to settle his contract and make an appearance. Reaves followed a few days later, but all-star slotback, Joe Poplawski, retired, finishing his role as a Winnipeg Blue Bomber.

"I think Pop and Cal were $10k apart on a new contract and both stood their ground," recalls Bauer. "Pop just retired and Cal replaced him. In sports, if you can find them younger, better and cheaper, sometimes that is the way it goes."

There was a distinct difference in the atmosphere of the 1987 training camp. This was Mike Riley's first camp as head coach and he was going to run it the way he wanted.

"You have to remember that Mike inherited a Cal Murphy football team of veterans. We were molded the way Cal wanted, so, we were much easier to coach. We didn't need much in the way of motivation because that was already in our blood."

"Cal's early camps were absolute horror shows," recalls Bauer. "He would run us into the ground and tried to break you. Those who broke, left. Those who didn't, stayed. So Mike's camps were much easier, but the tone for the team had already been set."

Just days before the CFL's regular season was set to kick off, the Montreal Alouettes folded, forcing the league to realign the divisions. The Winnipeg Blue Bombers would now compete in the Eastern Division.

In their first season in the Eastern Division, the 1987 Winnipeg Blue Bombers finished in 1st place with an impressive 12–6 record. But on Sunday November 22, a sell-out crowd at Winnipeg Stadium watched as the Toronto Argonauts embarrassed their Blue Bombers 19-3 in the Eastern Final game. It was termed as the Blue Bombers' flattest performance of the season.

"We shit the bed in that game. It's that simple," said Bauer. "In '87, we were probably one of the most talented teams in the league, but fell short against a hungrier Argo team in the playoffs. And because of that, the entire '87 season is still a sore point for me to this day. I think we may have believed the headlines and in professional sports, you just can't let that happen."

Chapter Seven

... a club that has seldom played well and never yet dominated a game in every aspect.
...offence non-existent
...bargain basement Bombers.

Those comments were not leftovers from the Winnipeg Blue Bombers' 1987. They were published by local Winnipeg media, nine games into the '88 season. The Blue Bombers were 4-5 and had just suffered an embarrassing 29-19 loss against the Saskatchewan Roughriders.

"From day one of that season we had many roster changes and some of them were in critical positions," said Bauer. "We knew it was going to be a year of change and challenge."

Seventy players showed up to the '88 training camp to compete for 36 positions in mid-June. CFL officials had adjusted team's game rosters that year to consist of 20 Non Imports, 14 Imports and 2 Quarterbacks. The reserve list was lowered from 4 players to 2 players. In addition, if a team decided to dress 14 Imports, one of those imports had to be designated as a special teams' player.

But what truly over shadowed the news was not who showed up, but who didn't. The Blue Bombers were missing their number one quarterback, running back, wide receiver and linebacker.

In early May, quarterback Tom Clements decided it was time to retire. Another four month separation from his family in Chicago seemed to be too much and became his deciding factor. Now Blue Bombers' Head Coach Mike Riley, would be heading into his second season without an experienced quarterback. Back-up Tom Muecke had seen limited playing time behind Clements and had not earned the confidence of his coach.

In the previous season, the Winnipeg Football Club had spent $2,883,929 on player's salaries, exceeding the league limit of $2.8 million. As punishment, the league had imposed a fine on the club of $16,785. In 1988, teams were only allowed to spend a total of $3 million on their entire football operations with $2.3 dedicated towards player salaries. General Manager, Cal Murphy had some difficult decisions to make.

Running back Willard Reaves and wide receiver Jeff Boyd were both holding out because of contract disputes with Murphy. Murphy and Reaves could not come to terms over his contract despite several weeks of talks. Scheduled to receive $165,000, Murphy wanted to cut Reaves salary back to between $85,000 and $100,000. Reaves would be released in July after 62 games with the Blue Bombers. He piled up 5923 rushing yards, 1202 receiving yards and 55 touchdowns. Losing the four time divisional all-star, three-time All Canadian, and the CFL's top player in 1984, left a big hole to fill.

Jeff Boyd, the team's leading receiver at $95,000 could also not come to terms with Murphy and was traded to the Argonauts before the season opener. Murphy had decided to again go with younger talent with less salary expectations.

On defense, the Blue Bombers' stand-out linebacker, Tyrone Jones had made the decision to explore opportunities in the NFL in the '87 off season. Jones was a four-time CFL and five-time division All-Star. He still holds the Winnipeg career sack record of 98, along with Grey Cup records for most sacks in a game (four) and most career Grey Cup sacks (five). He had won the CFL's Most Outstanding Defensive Player Award in 1985 and was on the winning Grey Cup team in 1984. He also won the Grey Cup MVP in 1984.

"Holdouts during camp really weren't that big of a deal to the rest of us," said Bauer. "But if they extended into the regular season, it could possibly hurt us as a team. You also start to wonder how committed the player is to the team. Don't get me wrong, we all have to look after ourselves and our families. Many of us could have gone and played elsewhere for more money, but didn't take that option because of what we had as a team. I felt as a true team player, you have responsibilities to your brothers on that team."

Two cost saving measures were also put in place for the '88 training camp. The late start – mid June instead of late May and for the first time, players with homes in Winnipeg wouldn't have to stay at the team hotel. Murphy was hoping the latter would save the team $5,000.

"We lost quite a few players that year and we were still missing that key quarterback that makes things tick," said Bauer.

But what didn't change during '88 training camp was the overall makeup of the Blue Bombers' offensive line. Bauer, at center was back with David Black at left tackle, Chris Walby at right tackle, Nick Bastaja at left guard and Bob Molle at right guard. Backing them up was Brad Tierney and Steve Rodehutskors.

"I was finally able to settle into one position," said Bauer. "The center is really involved in the schemes, audibles and on field calls to set things up for everyone else."

"Defenses changed with motion and that meant blocking schemes changed as well requiring split second decisions and communications to the entire offense and quarterback. I was good at that and the guys knew I would get them the information they needed to complete their assignments."

"From a physical standpoint, Cal had the center do things that no other team asked. You were left on an island a lot of times. He also had the center pull different directions. Try that with your arm between your legs while ensuring the quarterback got the ball cleanly. But I was able to step up and meet all of those challenges."

"Even with the changes, what was consistent was the core of our team," said Bauer. "And believe me, we did take exception to those media comments."

Just nine days after the start of training camp, Coach Riley dressed 45 players for the team's first preseason game against the Saskatchewan Roughriders. Coach Riley left 14 starters in Winnipeg, leaving him with only 20 players who had ever played for the Blue Bombers before. Among the 45, Riley had three quarterbacks; veteran Joe Paopao, third year back-up, Tom Muecke and rookie Jeff Telford.

"We had a lot of quarterbacks come and go that season," said Bauer. "I learned a lot from them. I had to pay really close attention to each one so I could be more effective in my job and particularly with the less experienced quarterbacks."

The first outing was an embarrassing 41-6 loss that left Coach Riley with more questions than answers. To make things even more confusing, on July 2nd, the team released veteran quarterback Joe Paopao. His release was not based on his performance in the preseason game, but because of another contract dispute between Murphy and Paopao's agent, Gil Scott.

The Blue Bombers would go on to split the final two preseason games 1-1 against Ottawa and Toronto.

"Molle ripped his knee ligaments in the loss to Ottawa," said Bauer. "That was a hit we didn't need. There was enough confusion already and uncertainty surrounding the team." Second year back-up, Steve Rodehutskors would be activated into duty as the starting right guard.

When all was said and done, the Blue Bombers roster turnover from the 1987 season was 28 players. At the quarterback position, Riley had made his decision. Bauer and his line mates would be protecting either Roy Dewalt, a veteran picked up from the B.C. Lions as their starter, or back-up, Tom Muecke going into the regular season.

The first regular season game was against their long-time rivals, the B.C. Lions. It was billed as a quarterback duel between the Bombers Roy Dewalt and the B.C. Lion's new quarterback, Matt Dunigan. But the game did not live up to its billing by any means. Dunigan's offense racked up 46 points against a beaten up Blue Bombers' defense. The entire Blue Bombers offense sputtered by adding only 3 points to the scoreboard the entire game.

In the following game against the Hamilton Tiger-Cats, they again struggled during the opening few minutes. Starter Roy Dewalt was pulled in favour of back-up Tom Muecke who would inspire the team to a 21-9 win.

But that inspiration wouldn't carry them through to the next game against the Saskatchewan Roughriders. Dewalt, Muecke and the entire Blue Bombers' offense fell flat in another embarrassing loss of 46-18.

An arm injury to starter Dewalt would put Meucke in the driver's seat in an early season rematch against the B.C. Lions and Meucke led the Bombers to a 38-21 win.

But then things started moving backwards again. Two losses would come at the hands of the Ottawa Rough Riders and Edmonton Eskimos in the following weeks.

Sitting at 2-4, this would become the Blue Bombers worst start of the 80s. With one third of the season over, an immediate turnaround was needed to save the season.

Riley made the decision to start Tom Meucke against the Roughriders on August 31 and he led the team to a quick 24-11 lead by the halfway point in the game. But the Blue Bombers fell apart in the second half, allowing the Roughriders an opportunity to take the game away. And they would have if it hadn't been for a heroic effect by Meucke to take the Bombers down the field in the last 90 seconds for a score.

But the Roughriders would take their revenge the following week, beating the Blue Bombers 29-19.

"We really struggled offensively. We knew that our defense was outstanding and in previous years it had been the opposite," said Bauer.

At the end of the previous season, the Blue Bombers' offensive line was ranked as the best unit in the Canadian Football League, but in 1988, they had not lived up to their status. Coach Riley took a hard look at the line as a whole. He was not satisfied in the play of centre Bauer and tackles Walby and Black. The preseason loss of Bob Molle had forced Steve Rodehutskors to step in, but he proved that he was not quite ready for the task. In response, Riley pulled him from his starting position. Nick Bastaja proved to be the club's steadiest lineman, but the entire unit was being blamed for the 41 quarterback sacks in the opening nine games of the season. That compared to just 42 sacks in the entire '87 season.

"Sacks aren't always the fault of the O-Lline," said Bauer. "The quarterback may hold onto the ball to long, he rolls out of the pocket, backs miss their blocks, reads are missed by the receivers, etc. But the line takes all that heat."

"We were determined to show people that we were different, but we also knew we had challenges in several areas. We weren't the dominant team of talent as we were the year before."

"We knew we were a good line," said Walby. "You're expected to do your job and we had high expectations of each other and of ourselves. I remember Mike Riley telling me "Don't ever point a finger at someone else because you'll have three pointing at you."

"The intensity at times in the locker room was crazy. Lyle, Blackie and me were definitely the leaders," said Walby. "But we heard it when we let the team down. I remember Rod Hill coming into the dressing room at halftime and screaming 'You guys suck!' Then all of a sudden a fight broke out. This happened all the time in the dressing room. But when the whistle blew, we would get back on the field as a team. The way we all got along was unbelievable. I think it was because we had been together for so long and we had a common goal."

"I remember it was around that time there was a picture in the paper where we all stood with paper bags on our heads with a headline, 'No Respect' or something like that," said Bauer. "We were the 'Rodney Dangerfields' of the CFL."

"I loved all that negative press," said James West. "It made me want to go out hard the next game, just to shut them all up."

"I remember some guy in '87 wrote that I had as much impact as a 'dollop of whipped cream on Jello,'" laughs West. "He even called me 'Mild West.' But trust me, that guy shut up after the next game."

The critics did start to notice when the combination of Dewalt and Muecke used newcomer running back, Tim Jessie to pick apart the B.C. Lions in an impressive 34-8 win.

"It was Bauer and those guys on the line," said Tim Jessie. "They really made my job easy. I just had to hold back and look for the holes they made."

But just 6 days after their soundest offensive showing of the season, the Blue Bombers put another one in the loss column, losing 20-14 against the Calgary Stampeders. Quarterback Roy Dewalt was put on the trading block, then placed on the reserve list where he collected a game cheque of nearly $7000 per game.

Tom Muecke was positioned as the Blue Bombers' starting quarterback with a new addition, Sean Salisbury as his back-up. 24 year-old Salisbury had been a standout with USC and had spent time with the Indianapolis Colts in the NFL.

On their next game against Ottawa, Salisbury would replace Muecke in the first five minutes and lead the team to a stunning 31-0 win.

Six days later, in Saskatchewan, Tom Meucke developed a swollen bursa sac in his right elbow during the pre-game warm-up. With three minutes to kick-off, Coach Riley named Salisbury as their starting quarterback. CFL rules stated at the time, any roster changes had to be made one hour before kick-off and had to be league approved. Because of that rule, the Blue Bombers would be forced to play the game without a back-up quarterback. It was now even more crucial that the offensive line step up their game and protect the team's only quarterback. The Blue

Bombers would go on to beat the Roughriders, 32-20. The offensive line controlled the Riders pass rush and allowed just 3 sacks the entire game. The Blue Bombers were now 7-6 and tied for second with the Hamilton Tiger-Cats.

With the uncertainty of Muecke's injury, the Blue Bombers activated Roy Dewalt as back-up announcing Salisbury as the starter against the Edmonton Eskimos.

One week later, with Muecke healthy, Roy Dewalt was released by the team. "Roy was a great talent in B.C.," said Bauer. "I don't know if our schemes were different or his time had come. He was a great guy and I had wished it could have turned out better for him."

Sean Salisbury would go on to lead the Blue Bombers on a four game winning streak and putting them into contention for a playoff position with a record of 9-6. "We seemed to settle into a rhythm," said Bauer. "But then we lost three in a row."

Back to back losses against the Argos and a final regular season loss against the Lions put the Bombers' season at 9-9, barely making the playoffs.

"We lost Chris in that last Hamilton win," said Bauer about his linemate Chris Walby. "Salisbury also missed that last game against the Lions because of sore ribs and we were underdogs again."

With Walby out with a partial tear in the medial ligament of his right knee, back-up lineman, Steve Rodehutskors was called back into action.

There are usually two seasons in any sports league; the regular season and the playoffs. Playoffs can mean a fresh start for a team and the 1988 Blue Bombers embraced the second chance that was placed in front of them.

"Regardless of what people were saying about us, we were still tight as a unit and we stuck together," said Bauer. "In spite of what people said, we still believed."

In the Eastern Division Semi Final, against a seasoned Hamilton team, the Blue Bombers beat the Tiger-Cats, 35-28 to advance to the Eastern Finals against the Argonauts.

On paper, the numbers were stacked against the Blue Bombers. They had lost twice to the Toronto Argonauts that season who had finished in first place with a record of 14-4.

There wasn't much hope. The Blue Bombers were a .500 team at best, barely finishing in third place. "Nobody thought it was possible," said Walby. "We were definitely the underdogs going into that game."

"Almost everyone counted us out before we even hit the field," said Bauer. "Chris was out, we had an inexperienced quarterback and Toronto had the momentum going into that game."

But the Blue Bombers would come out of the block quickly, building a 11-0 lead at the end of the first quarter. They would close out the first half 11-3 and by the time the game was over, the underdog Blue Bombers had upset the first place Argonauts, 27-11. They claimed the '88 CFL Eastern Division championship and earned a spot in the 76th Grey Cup game.

One week after their shocking win against the Argos, the Winnipeg Blue Bombers were ready to face the B.C. Lions in Ottawa in the Grey Cup. Once again the Blue Bombers were labelled as the underdog. The Lions were another team that had the momentum on their side. Their veteran quarterback, Matt Dunigan, had a banner year leading his team to a 10-8 record.

"We went in with a plan," said Bauer. "Sean Salisbury had to play within his ability to be successful. We had to run a fairly simple offense and make no mistakes. And then let the defense take care of the rest of the business," said Bauer.

The B.C. Lions would take an early 7-1 lead in the opening quarter on a Matt Dunigan handoff to running back Anthony Cherry, scoring on a 14-yard run. The Blue Bombers, Trevor Kennerd kicked a 22-yard field goal, pulling the Blue Bombers within one point.

In the second quarter, Kennerd tied the score with a 43-yard field goal. But shortly after that, B.C. quarterback Matt Dunigan would fire a pass to David Williams to connect on a 26-yard scoring play, giving the Lions a 14-7 advantage.

The Blue Bombers refused to go down without a fight and on their next possession, Sean Salisbury threw a 35-yard touchdown strike to James Murphy to tie the game.

B.C.'s Lui Passaglia would fail on a 41-yard field goal attempt near the end of the first half, but the safety gave the Lions a 15-14 lead at halftime.

"We knew we were in tough against a more talented offensive team, but we also knew our defense could match their offense. On numerous occasions in that game I would tell Sean Salisbury what to audible and what he had to do."

In the third quarter, the Lions' Passaglia and the Blue Bombers' Kennerd exchanged field goals to tie the game, 19-19 heading into the final fifteen minutes.

With 2:55 remaining in the game, Trevor Kennerd kicked a 30-yard field goal to put the Bombers in front for the first time in the game. With the score 22-19 in favour of the Blue Bombers, Dunigan led the Lions 75 yards down to the Blue Bombers ten -yard line.

"We were an 'us against the world' team and to hell with what people said or thought," said Bauer.

With a first and goal on the ten-yard line, Dunigan stepped back to hand off to his running back Anthony Cherry. Cherry worked his way to the Winnipeg seven-yard line with 1:45 left in the game.

"I remember that next play like it was yesterday," said Bauer. "On that drive, I remember kneeling on the sidelines thinking we can't let this slip away. This was it. Since 1982 I had worked for this. For seven years, I had gotten my ass kicked and I had kicked my share as well. I had been forced out with injuries. I played with injuries. I had sacrificed myself and my family for that moment."

On the next play, Dunigan dropped back and looked to the end zone for an open receiver. He threw the ball towards the corner of the end zone, but his pass would be tipped at the line of scrimmage by the out stretched arms of linebacker, Delbert Fowler. The ball floated through the air and was intercepted in the end zone by Winnipeg's Mike Gray.

"Sure enough. The 'Tree,' Delbert Fowler tips Dunigan's pass, Michael catches it, runs out of the end zone and falls to the ground. After that it looked like West was beating the shit out of him. He wasn't. He was celebrating. His arms were swinging like a mad man."

The Blue Bombers had stopped their long-time rivals at the gate.

On the next two plays, the B.C. defense held the Blue Bombers on their own three yard line. On third down, Mike Riley elected to give up a safety in favour of better field position, cutting the margin to just one.

"After that the offense just needed to hold our ground, protect the ball and rely on the kicking leg of Bob Cameron and our special teams."

The ensuing Bob Cameron kick-off was returned by B.C.'s Anthony Drawhorn for 38 yards to the B.C. 45-yard line, but the ball was brought back to the 30 when Cherry was flagged on a rough play penalty. The B.C. Lions couldn't get anything going and the Winnipeg Blue Bombers held on to win the 76th Grey Cup, 22-21.

"I remember standing with the rest of guys from the O-Line and having a couple cold ones at centerfield long after everyone had left the stadium," recalls Bauer. "We didn't want that moment to ever end. We had worked damn hard to get there. I couldn't imagine that there could be any better feeling than winning that Cup."

Chapter Eight

With dire financial concerns throughout the CFL still looming, the Blue Bombers opened their 1989 training camp on a sour note. Sean Salisbury was in a contract dispute with GM, Cal Murphy.

Murphy had offered the quarterback a one year deal with a salary of just over $80,000 but Salisbury wanted security. The B.C. Lions had secured Matt Dunigan for $225,000 per season and Roy Dewalt was collecting $175,000 from the Ottawa Rough Riders. Salisbury felt he was in the same league as them and wanted more. The average salary for an experienced quarterback in 1989 was $96,000.

"I knew there was a contract riff between him and Cal," said Bauer. "And that never ends well. I think he saw himself as the winner of the Grey Cup and deserved all the credit. But we knew it was the defense and special teams that gave us a chance and I don't think Sean wanted to acknowledge that."

Salisbury was determined to gain some security at least until the 1991 season, but Murphy was holding his ground. He was confident he could win with his current quarterback trio of Tom Muecke, Lee Saltz and Sammy Garza. Salisbury was not a hold- out, but he was definitely unhappy.

Bauer had reached an agreement in terms on his '89 contract before training camp opened. He was now in his eighth year with the Blue Bombers and his fourth season as the starting centre. He was also the club's nominee for the 1988 Schenley Award as the CFL's top offensive lineman.

"It was pretty cool being able bring the Grey Cup to school to show all my friends for show and tell," said daughter, Danni.

Chris Walby had signed a three year deal with no raise in his salary in the off season. "I told Cal I wanted a vacation. He just handed me a Travel Manitoba brochure," said Walby who had explored his options in the NFL but decided to remain with the club. Nick Bastaja was retiring so Murphy needed Walby for stability on the offensive line.

David Black, who had also re-signed his contract, was asked to move to Bastaja's spot at guard between Bauer and Rodehutskors. Walby and Molle would complete the line with Brad Tierney and Dave Vankoughnett backing up their positions.

But, out of the blue, quarterback Tom Muecke announced his retirement in the early days of training camp. "Football is no longer fun," he stated to the local media. "I dreaded practice."

In the opening regular season game against Ottawa, Chris Walby strained the knee ligaments in his left knee. Black was moved to tackle and Tierney and Vankoughnett would alternate in his spot. In August, Tierney was traded with defensive lineman Willie Fears to Ottawa for offensive guard, Nick Benjamin. In his rookie season, Benjamin was named the East Rookie of the Year and runner up as the CFL Most Outstanding Rookie.

"That, again, was a tough year trying to find the right pieces," said Bauer. By mid-September the team was 7-4, following their latest win against the B.C. Lions.

But that would be it for the Blue Bombers. They went on a six game losing streak that was unmatched in the '80s. On November 2nd, Sean Salisbury was placed on recallable waivers, the first step in granting him his outright release. Salisbury had been sharply criticized during the losing streak for throwing far too many interceptions. His agent called out Cal Murphy in the local media, stating, "a gutless GM that made a gutless move."

"I liked Sean," said Bauer "But always got the impression that the CFL wasn't for him. He played to huge crowds in college and I believe he thought the NFL was his deserved destiny."

In the final game of the season, Lee Saltz was named the starter and Sammy Garza as designated as the back-up. The Blue Bombers would end up on the losing end of that game against Ottawa 24-10. It was their seventh straight loss, but they still had a spot in the playoffs.

Heading into the Eastern Semi Final against the Toronto Argonauts, there was concern over the Blue Bombers' sputtering offense. Quarterback Lee Saltz was still unproven in just his second start. But the team's solid defense kept the Argonauts offense subdued, giving the Blue Bombers a shocking 30-7 victory and a trip to the Eastern Final.

But this was not going to be another Cinderella season for the Blue Bombers. Against the Hamilton Tiger-Cats the following week, they would go down in a 14-10 defeat.

"In the Eastern Final we really struggled," said Bauer. "And so did Trevor Kennerd, missing several field goals. I believe if he would have made one we would have advanced to the Grey Cup game. But no game is ever won or lost by one player or on one play."

"Let's face it, guys like me, Lyle, Blackie, we had had that taste of winning," said Walby. "Once you taste that fruit of being the best, you desperately want to keep it."

"It was a very tough season and I hated losing. We all did," said Bauer. "That ankle gave me significant problems. I missed a few games because of that and I probably shouldn't have played later in the year or during the playoffs. As a team, there seemed to be something missing in '89."

Before the year was over, GM Cal Murphy went to work on his 1990 team. He had agreed to terms on his own contract, giving the Blue Bombers another three years and he immediately set things in motion.

After two years of negotiations, Murphy had finally come to an agreement with quarterback Danny McManus. The former Florida State Seminole first caught Murphy's attention in January of 1988, but they could never come to terms with his agent. McManus was now acting as his own agent after an unsuccessful stint with the Kansas City Chiefs of the NFL and agreed to join the Blue Bombers for the 1990 season. But he was still not the experienced player Murphy was looking for.

In Saskatchewan, an unhappy Tom Burgess wanted out of the Roughriders organization. Burgess, the CFL's leading quarterback in the opening half of the 1989 season had been relegated to the back-up position behind Kent Austin. Murphy had had an interest in Burgess at one time, but that seemed to die off as soon as Doug Flutie became a free agent.

Murphy had insisted he was happy with his four quarterbacks; Garza, Saltz, McManus and Brent Pease, despite making four attempts to sign Flutie. Tom Burgess had a high price and Murphy was not willing to give up cornerback Rod Hill or linebacker Greg Battle.

But things change quickly in the football business. On July 2, when Murphy couldn't swing a deal for Doug Flutie, Tom Burgess was traded to Winnipeg for Lee Saltz and a third-round draft pick.

Tom Burgess was 26-years-old with four years' experience in the Canadian Football League. He was originally signed by Ottawa in 1986 after graduating from Colgate University. He was a member of the Ottawa Rough Riders in 1986 before moving to the Saskatchewan Roughriders from 1987-89.

"To us, Tom Burgess was really the second coming of Tom Clements," said Bauer. "He had similar body type, similar arm, and similar demeanor, to a point.

"I had arrived in Winnipeg during training camp after two-a-days had already ended," recalls Burgess. "I didn't really meet anyone until that first afternoon practice. Lyle had an infectious laugh with a clean-shaven face and an articulate manner, especially compared to some of the other hoodlum-biker-gang-looking linemen like David Black and Chris Walby. These guys were by far the biggest bunch of animals of any line in the league. Nick Benjamin was huge with the thickest chest I probably had ever seen. Rodie was a naturally big farm-boy-looking guy. Bob Molle was a tough nut, kind of like the shirtless crazy-man bald guy in the old Burt Reynolds' movie, 'The Longest Yard.' Lyle, on the other hand, while rather large and stocky, as to be expected, was more upstanding, business-like as I recall, which might explain his move to the front office later."

"I was glad to be in Winnipeg," said Burgess. "Playing against them was always a bit scary. When they were your adversaries, it was easy to drum up a little hate for Ty Jones and James West. Hell, they wanted you to hate them. But when they were your teammates, they were the very best."

"I hated having those big guys on me all the time," said Burgess. "Michael Gray was one of those guys. We were playing against Winnipeg on the old Taylor field where I was crushed between his big fast moving body and the Taylor field turf which was like landing on indoor/outdoor carpet laid on a concrete floor. I missed half of a season with a broken collar bone because of him. Thanks Mike! He did say he was sorry when I joined the team."

"That season was a story book," said Bauer. "We led the Eastern Division from the first game and never looked back. It was probably the most complete team we ever had during my playing years. Tom was a great competitor. He was by far the toughest quarterback I ever played with. Very smart and, again, a huge competitor. He fit in well with the team. That trade was one of the smartest moves Cal ever made."

The first regular season game was a good indication of things to come. Against the Ottawa Rough Riders, the Bombers trailed 17-7 at the half. But the offensive line dominated the second half with Chris Walby, Nick Benjamin, Bauer, Steve Rodehutskors and Bob Molle lined up in front of Tom Burgess.

"Those were big backsides to be behind," said Burgess. "But, trust me, I wanted it that way. The only problem was that those guys were all so big and tall, most of the time I couldn't see downfield."

"Tom really earned the respect of all of the linemen really fast," said Bauer. "Never once did he blame a lineman for a sack even though sometimes we got beat clean. He would always say it was his fault."

'Those guys were pretty opinionated too, especially Walby," said Burgess recalling the early days of the 1990 season. "He would gladly have taken the play calling duties from me, and trust me I let him do it often enough. But keep in mind, with Walby, anyone can guess what he called, "Run the f#@*ing ball behind me, goddammit!"

By mid-season, the Blue Bombers were 6-3 with a firm hold on first place in the Eastern Division. Despite some early season struggles, Burgess was starting to grasp his leadership role on the team.

"Lyle was an important mediator when our emotions got hot," recalls Burgess. "I remember once, a rare instance, when I was sacked often in a game against the Roughriders on Labour Day. It was a lopsided affair and not in our favour, one of those hot as hell days in Regina. After one of the many sacks, I probably got up a little hot and maybe said something, I don't know. Rodie decided to retort with "If you wouldn't hold on to the damn ball for so damn long!" Well, that kind of pissed me off until Lyle, who heard it, laughed his ass off, a big hearty laugh and the heat dissipated. And if I don't remember it quite right, forgive me; because I did get hit a lot that day. But in any case that is the kind of thing Lyle could do and then everyone else was in favour of laughing as well. As the center, he had everyone's respect; he was the Captain of that line."

"We knew we had something special going on and we were all committed to completing the objective," said Bauer. "Our offense was explosive, the special teams were great, and that defense was absolutely insane. Tom was not only fitting in, he was leading."

"In professional football, maybe even more so in the CFL, fans are often fixated on the talents of a quarterback or an especially gifted receiver or runner," said Burgess. "No doubt such talent is important and there has to be production from those positions. Where would we have been without Mimbs or Perry or Houser or Streater? But if a team is built to win consistently, it is because of the strengths of a stalwart defense and dominating offensive line; blocking and tackling. This had defined the Winnipeg Blue Bombers of that era; a big bruising offensive line and scary trash-talking in-your-face defense."

"I was only too happy to be the plug-and-play quarterback that got to work behind them. So, if they are considered to be the best all-time line, I won't argue that because they were great and I loved being their teammate. It was truly because of the stalwart play of those main cogs, like Lyle and Chris and Blackie."

"Good O-Lines tend to be close knit and this one was no exception," said Burgess. "We had regular after-practice meet-ups. It was the O-Line, myself and a few others who would meet after practice at Mario's. I should also add Warren Hudson was always there, too. He was, as a fullback, an honorary lineman of the first order and we all enjoyed each other. That was an important thing. We liked to spend time together. We'd have a few drinks and laugh at each other, but that O-Line was the cornerstone of that chemistry."

That chemistry, talent and pure determination carried the Blue Bombers to finish the season with a record of 12-6 season and seated the team in first place in the East. In the Eastern Semi Final, the second place Toronto Argonauts would go on to defeat the Ottawa Rough Riders 34-25, and advance to play Winnipeg in the final.

The Blue Bombers would once again face Matt Dunigan in a crucial playoff game. But this time he was in an Argonauts' uniform. Dunigan would go down in defeat 20-17 against Burgess and the Blue Bombers.

That win meant the Winnipeg Blue Bombers were headed to the 78th Grey Cup against West Division Champions, the Edmonton Eskimos.

Early in the first quarter, Eskimos' quarterback, Tracy Ham, drove Edmonton from their own 32-yard line to the Winnipeg 16. After a procedure penalty, Ham's pass would be intercepted by the Blue Bombers' linebacker Greg Battle at the 1 yard line and returned to the Edmonton 43. Tom Burgess would lead his team to the Edmonton 14-yard line, but could not score the touchdown, as his pass was knocked down by Brett Williams. Trevor Kennard kicked a 14-yard field goal to put Winnipeg in the lead 3-0.

Edmonton's Blake Marshall would fumble on the Eskimo's 45-yard line, leading the Blue Bombers to score a touchdown.

At the end of the quarter Winnipeg running back Robert Mimbs fumbled, giving Edmonton possession on their own 43-yard line. They were unable to take advantage of the turnover but scored a 56-yard single on Ray Macoritti's punt.

Neither offense was able to mount a sustained drive until the end of the quarter, when Ham got the Eskimos to the Bomber 37-yard line. They had to settle for a Macoritti field goal on the last play of the half, making the halftime score 10-4 in favour of the Blue Bombers.

But early in the second half, Greg Battle made his second interception and returned it 34 yards for a touchdown.

Shortly after, Burgess completed a 55-yard pass to Perry Tuttle, who was tackled on the Edmonton 5. Two plays later, Tuttle would make a fingertip catch at the goal line, for another touchdown.

The next two plays summarized that 1990 Grey Cup game. With less than five minutes left in the third quarter, the Blue Bombers' had a healthy 24-4 lead. On a third and ten, Blue Bombers' punter, Bob Cameron, kicked the ball downfield to Edmonton's Henry "Gizmo" Williams. Williams caught the ball at the Eskimo's 5-yard line. The 185lb punt returner was immediately surrounded by Nick Benjamin (270lb), James West (220lb), and Tyrone Jones (220lb). Three steps into his return, Williams was stripped of the ball and Jones scooped it up.

On the next play, quarterback Tom Burgess would throw a screen pass just a few yards out to fullback, Warren Hudson, on the 17-yard line. The powerback fell in behind Bauer and Rodehutskors for an easy touchdown.

While the Blue Bombers' defense kept the Eskimos' offense off balance for the rest of the entire game, Burgess and the offense racked up the final score, 50-11.

"That Grey Cup game was a complete shit-kicking in all areas," said Bauer. "I don't think I have ever witnessed a more dominant display by a linebacker than Greg Battle. It was amazing to watch and still, to this day, I am mesmerized by that interception he made over the top of the Eskimo's fullback."

"There was no looking back in that game. Hammer down and a foot on their throats from the onset and there was no backing off. No mercy."

"I do remember facing Brett 'The Toaster' Williams in that game, who was one of the best in the league. But that was to be our day and personally, that was my day against one of the best."

"That team's championship caliber was due to that O-Line and those pillars of the defense like James West, Tyrone Jones, and Greg Battle," said Burgess.

"I can still see Lyle reclining by his locker, knee braces unhinged, with a big smile on his face," said Burgess. "And I can hear Walby in the background loudly sharing a funny story about a play or something that happened during the game. I think most of us would tell you, we miss the locker room atmosphere and those moments the most."

Chapter Nine

After his rookie year in 1982, Lyle had returned to Saskatoon to not only hit the weights, but he hit the books as well. "I wasn't just a pretty face. I was smart enough to know that football could end at any time," he said. "Cuts, injuries, you name it, the thought was always in the back of my mind. There were too many factors out of my control in football and I needed to have a back-up plan. Real estate had always interested me."

By 1983, Bauer had successfully obtained his real estate licence, but having a licence is only one step in the process. Finding a position at an established brokerage firm is another.

"I believe it was someone at the Blue Bombers' office that first told me about Neal Fisher at Block Bros," recalls Bauer. "I knew they were one of the top offices in the city so, I figured, why not."

"I remember the day he came to see me," said Neal Fisher, the broker/manager for Block Bros in southwest Winnipeg. In the 80's, Fisher had attracted some of the top real estate professionals in Winnipeg. Such well-known agents like Gary Bachman, Ed Dale, Glen Harvey and

Frank Saniuk among others, had all started their careers under Fisher's mentorship.

"We had been the top office not only in Winnipeg, but across Western Canada for a number of years. I wanted Lyle working with us, but unfortunately, he didn't meet the full licensing requirements because of his football career."

The Manitoba Real Estate Association stipulates that licenced real estate agents must be full time. A licenced agent cannot have any outside sources of income.

"At first, I had no choice. I had to turn him down. Because of those rules, his football career was definitely in the way," said Fisher. "But after some thought, and several meetings with the Winnipeg Real Estate Board, we found a way to accommodate him. Lyle's real estate licence would have to be suspended when the football season started, then reinstated when the season ended. Football players were compensated for the duration of the season only and it couldn't be considered an annual salary."

"From day one, Bowser meant business," said Walby. "He always had deals on the go and his pager drove me nuts. I was like, Lyle turn the fricken thing off, man. 'I can't,' he'd say. 'I might miss a call and then I'm screwed.'"

"Lyle was a good addition to our organization," said Fisher. "He added a lot to our office. He was dedicated and determined, but I have to admit, I did have some problems with him. He was stubborn. The main issue I had was him complying with our dress code. I had put a very strict dress code policy in place; dress pants, a collared shirt and tie at all times when they were in the office."

"Well, one day Lyle comes in after a workout. He's in a T-shirt with, of course no sleeves, shorts and sandals. I called him into my office and read him the policy," recalls Fisher. "He stood in the doorway of my office, this big hulking, 250lb figure and said, 'Fish, I was looking for a job when I found this one. I could go look again.' Then, he just turned and walked away."

"Then there was the time we had an office pool party and he picked me up and threw me in the pool; suit, shoes and all. But that's another story."

"Of course Kim and I used Lyle to find our home," said teammate David Black. "He really knew his stuff."

"I think Lyle's toughest client was my wife Margaret," recalls former General Manager, Paul Robson. "Lyle had found us a home in Charleswood when we came back to Winnipeg that we really loved. He told us the asking price; I think it was just over $200,000. But Margaret refused to go that high. After a few heated discussions with her, Margaret got her way and we got our new home."

"When I had to withdraw my license during football season, Heidi stepped up, got her license and took over my business during those months. She did that in addition to taking care of our kids and everything else. She did a great job."

But success in real estate sales still wasn't enough for Bauer. During the off-season of 1989, he had started pursuing his broker's licence which meant another round of intense educational courses. While others studied the playbook, Bauer focused on contract law and trust accounts.

"I remember one time we were on an eastern swing in 1990 and I was in the middle of my accounting course. Of course I couldn't attend the classes so I had them agree to let me write the exam without attending. They said there was no way I would pass it," said Bauer. "But I studied my ass off while we were staying a week in Burlington and I aced it. It surprised everyone at the Manitoba Real Estate Association."

In January 1991, Neal Fisher moved up to be become the district manager for all the Block Bros, offices in Winnipeg. One of his first appointments was placing Lyle Bauer as the broker/manager of their southwest office.

"That was the first time I saw him take over an organization," said Walby. "He believed he was cleaning house. There was no hesitation. His attitude was that he needed to start fresh. He needed his own people. And that's when I realized, this guy's got it off the field as well. I started calling him 'The Cleaner.'"

"That's when he taught me that as much as you may think there's loyalty in business, there isn't," said Walby.

"There's no loyalty in business. There's only loyalty when you bring your own team in."

But despite his success in real estate, Bauer's own personal team loyalty would draw him into another season on the field with the Blue Bombers. After weeks of discussions with Heidi and his family, Bauer decided he still hadn't finished his job on the field and returned for his 10th season. "With Winnipeg hosting the Grey Cup in '91, I wanted to come back. We had a chance to do something special that year and it would have been a shame to miss it."

But to do so he had to temporally suspend his broker's licence. Neal Fisher would act as the official broker for Bauer's office and his title would change to promotions manager for the season.

At the Winnipeg Football Club's office, Head Coach, Mike Riley was handing in his resignation. Riley was heading south to take the head coaching position with the San Antonio Riders of the new World League of American Football.

On March 11, General Manager, Cal Murphy announced long-time friend and associate, Darryl Rogers would become the Winnipeg Blue Bombers' next head coach. Murphy and Rogers had worked together at San Jose State before Murphy had started his CFL career.

Darryl Rogers had been a controversial head coach for the Detroit Lions in the NFL for four years, compiling a less than stellar career record of 18–40. One of his more infamous quotes during his tenure with the Lions was when he once wondered aloud to reporters after a loss, "What does a coach have to do around here to get fired?" Several reports made reference to the fact that he had lost the respect of his players over time.

"I think Mike leaving had Cal scrambling a bit," said Bauer. "Cal and Mike always had a good working relationship. We knew there had been a relationship between Cal and Rogers in the past."

"Maybe Rogers was a decent coach at one time, but some of us learned quickly that he was really just putting in time. I never did understand why Cal hired him. He spent more time watching the golf channel in his office instead of watching game films."

"I remember the defensive coordinator Rogers brought in, Larry somebody, watching game films and being surprised by all of the on-field motion. He would say things like, 'That's illegal. They can't do that.' I knew we were in trouble."

The Winnipeg Blue Bombers opened their rookie training camp with the more players under contract than any other team in the league with 95 bodies. At that time, CFL rules stipulated that clubs were only allowed 65 players in camp, so several cuts after the rookie camp were inevitable.

When it was time for the veterans to report, restlessness had already spread through the locker room. The financial pressures of the entire league were affecting teams and the players. One of the more out spoken Blue Bombers'players, Tyrone Jones was demanding a new contract and eventually he walked out of training camp in frustration. He returned a few days later, empty handed and disappointed because Cal Murphy was not going to give in.

"Ty was one of those guys that pushed the boundaries with Cal," said Bauer. "He always had something to say and that didn't sit well with Cal. It didn't matter how good of an athlete you were, Cal had his limits."

The CFL as a whole was a financial mess, desperate for revenue. In early 1991, Harry Ornest had sold the Toronto Argonauts to Bruce McNall, owner of the NHL's Los Angeles Kings, Wayne Gretzky and comedian, John Candy. The group stunned the league with the signing of Raghib "Rocket" Ismail for an unheard of $18.2 million over four years. Mike "Pinball" Clemons and quarterback Matt Dunigan were also added to the Argos roster.

In July, the Board of Directors of the Ottawa Rough Riders resigned, causing the CFL to assume the ownership duties of that franchise. A new ownership group, Bernie and Lonie Glieberman from Detroit stepped up, expressing interest in purchasing the team, but not until the end of the '91 season and only after receiving assurances from the league they would not inherit any outstanding debt. The latter would have serious ramifications for the other nine teams.

Not only did the Ottawa franchise become a ward of the league, but their creditors were awarded more than $850,000. The team's debt included $725,584 to the province of Ontario for unpaid retail sales tax dating back to 1989, $94,741 to ex-head coach Bob Weber who had been fired in 1988 and $20,000 to Saxon Athletics.

In previous years, the CFL had negotiated the television rights for games. They would then distribute an equal share of that revenue to the individual teams. For example, in 1990 each team had received $650,000 as their share of the television rights revenue. But in 1991, the CFL , under Commissioner, J. Donald Crump, decided to purchase their own air time for games with the hopes of recouping the investment by selling advertising time on the telecasts. Despite their efforts, just keeping the Ottawa Rough Riders afloat for that season ate up most of the league's television revenue.

Three games into the season, the Blue Bombers were 1-2. After splitting back to back games with the Ottawa Rough Riders, it seemed like the Blue Bombers had gone flat. The offense was struggling and the defense seemed tired.

To shake things up, head coach Darryl Rogers replaced quarterback Tom Burgess with back-up Danny McManus against the winless Hamilton Tiger-Cats. But McManus' first CFL start was short lived. Just thirty minutes into the game, McManus suffered an injury to his right forearm and was replaced by Burgess. Burgess would lead the team to a narrow 25-24 victory.

The following next two weeks, the Blue Bombers would defeat the unbeaten Calgary Stampeders in a home and home series, 39-26 and 28-15.

But the team would split the next home and home series with the Saskatchewan Roughriders and lose against the B.C. Lions, leaving them with a 6-5 record going into the final stretch of the season. The inconsistency was starting to wear on the team and fingers were being pointed in almost every direction.

"We were a talented, but distracted team because of coaching and off-field issues," said Bauer. "The job of the head coach is to put the players in the best position to have success. Darryl and his staff didn't have a clue about the Canadian game and that frustrated players who were committed and understood the game. And we already knew what it took to be champions."

"At that point in the season there was no belief in the coaching staff," said Bauer. "Players started to freelance, doing their own thing on the field. Before we knew it, a bunch of little things became huge."

"Of course finances were always in the back of a guy's mind. We didn't make a lot financially, so getting to the playoffs always meant more money in our pockets and it was frustrating when we weren't all on the same page like we had been in previous seasons."

"As an example, Cal would always negotiate meals into the team's hotel arrangements when we were on the road. As you know, some buffets can be better than others," said Bauer. "I can't remember which trip it was, but the chicken they served was pink and that is what started it all. There was a pile-on effect by some players and Trevor Kennerd was a big one to jump on board. He and Cal never saw eye to eye, so this became a soap box for him."

Eventually, a six-man committee was formed with Tyrone Jones, Less Browne, Mike Gray, Perry Tuttle, Trevor Kennerd and Tom Burgess. After several meetings, the group drew up a list of grievances to be presented to the club's Board of Directors with Jones acting as the group's spokesman. According to some, the players said if a meeting with the Board was not granted, the team would consider boycotting the next game.

"Initially, this was just a group of players that weren't happy with their meals on the road and wanted the per diem instead," said Bauer.

"There were a lot of discussions," said James West. "But the bottom line was, we just wanted to be treated like professionals."

"I think after that incident it eventually lead to part or all of the per diem being paid and players were on their own for meals," said Bauer. "On one side, arranged meals served a couple of purposes. It ensured that players had the opportunity for decent nutrition and it kept us together as a team."

"But on the other side, some guys would rather have fast food and pocket the difference in cash which to me, was fine as well."

"But I also think that incident had an effect on our on-field performance and our exit from the playoffs," said Bauer. "From my standpoint, that just wasn't the right time to address those issues. Obviously, the thought and pressure put on the club in regards to a boycott was a strategy for some. But, for others, a potential boycott meant no paycheque and there wasn't a guy on that team who could really afford to miss one."

"In that instance, some players decided to assert control on and off the field which also lead to different agendas. Some wanted to win, while others were more focused on road meals. It caused some division in the locker room as there were very strong personalities on that team. Some of the guys were also coming to the end of the road and they knew it."

"It was a divisive exercise, not that the players side was wrong. It was the timing that was wrong and it did affect us in the locker room and on the field. It was dealt with properly in later years through collective bargaining between the CFL and CFLPA which resulted in per diems being paid and no meals provided."

"But, to be honest, there is a lot of truth that the club was being very frugal, but it had to be. I remember just before a game at Winnipeg Stadium, Robert Mimbs had to go across the street to buy his own socks. I am not sure that he really he had to, but he asked the equipment guy for a new pair and was declined. So he went and bought his own. I think part of it was to make a point and to provide him with his own soap box."

The informal player's group called another meeting at the clubhouse. Ted Bartman, the team's president, attended and heard the players' complaints. The Blue Bombers' players wanted a mediator appointed who would act as intermediary between the players and Cal Murphy. The meeting led to ironing out some of the minor problems, but the major issue still existed.

"Right from the start of the season, Darryl Rogers did not like Rod Hill. Rod is a different breed and had to be managed properly. Cal did it. Mike did it. But Darryl had no interest in it."

"A few days before an important game," said Bauer. "Rogers was going to bench Rod because he said something Darryl didn't like. To us, Rod was key to any victory and we needed him on the corner."

"I knew we had to have Rod to have a chance to win and I decided to stick my neck out. There was a lot of rumbling in the locker room about it and I talked to West before deciding to do something."

"I went to talk to Darryl, but all he could say was there had to be discipline and an example was going to be made. I told him he was taking away our chance of winning and we needed our best on the field. But he just wouldn't listen."

"His position was potentially taking money out of our pockets. We were not the highest paid roster in the league by far and we all counted on that playoff money to survive."

"I went to Cal and told him the same," said Bauer. "At first he stood behind Darryl's decision, but shortly after my discussion, Rod played. I think my influence made Cal go to Rogers to ensure Rod played."

"Hence, the real problem. We were a veteran team that had won a championship the year before and now we were now being led by a coach that didn't have the respect or confidence of the locker room."

Despite the turmoil, by the end of the regular season, the Blue Bombers record of 9-9 was still good enough to place them in second place in the East behind the Toronto Argonauts and earn them a playoff spot.

With home field advantage, the Blue Bombers would go on to beat the third place Ottawa Rough Riders 26-8, in the

East Semi Final. The win would set up another Winnipeg-Toronto battle for a spot in the Grey Cup game.

In Toronto, Argonauts owner Bruce McNall announced that he would triple his players' bonus money if they won the Grey Cup. At that time, the CFL would pay each player on the Grey Cup winning team a $12,000 bonus. McNall's offer would increase his players' bonus money to $36,000 each if the Argonauts won.

"That was tough," said Bauer. "The Argos were waving big cash around their players while at the same time, the community teams like us had to tighten their belts, just to keep the rest of the league afloat. "

In the East Final, the John Candy, Wayne Gretzky and Bruce McNall owned Argonauts, with Pinball, the Rocket and Matt Dunigan beat the Bombers 42-3. "They kicked our ass," said Bauer. "They were motivated and united with high profile ownership waving cash while we were focused on dissent, socks and partially cooked chicken."

"But that whole situation was a great lesson for me," said Bauer. "I saw first-hand that you need to keep players happy to the best of your ability. Nickel and diming them with the small things does as much damage as asking them for a pay cut. You are better off to hit one player with a pay cut than you are to piss off a whole team because of lousy road meals. It all comes down to respect."

"The savings on all that wouldn't have amounted to more than a couple of thousand dollars in the end, but it cost a lot more in team morale and on-field production."

"Those were things that players don't sometimes appreciate nor are they aware of. They were management issues and the role of management is to provide the best possible environment for the players so they could succeed."

"What happened in '91 needed to happen to make some corrections going into the future. Unfortunately it came at a cost, short term pain for long term gain. The key to our past success was that players believed in the coaching staff and management and vice versa. That relationship was fractured and in some cases it was beyond repair in '91."

"For me, I was done. It was time. I had thought about life after football from the first game I ever played. I always knew football was a fleeting vocation. You could be cut any time, injured or who knows what else that could end your career. I think that is what helped me become a long term thinker. I have always looked beyond tomorrow, next week, next year and that served me well."

"The decision and process was simple; I didn't want to be dragged off the field. I had watched too many other players' skills deteriorate. I had been forced off the field enough times, but this time it was going to be my decision even if it was before my time. I was making more money in the private sector than in football and my family was going to be fine.   Of course I wanted more championships, but I already had three Grey Cup rings. That's three more than most."

"I also learned that it takes a certain type of player to be successful in Winnipeg and to fit in. Most of us could have played somewhere else and made a lot more money. But the real payback was in Winnipeg where you could be part of a winner," said Bauer.

"I came to realize that years from now the money will be all gone," said Bauer. "But those rings and the memories would be with me forever. They were mine and I had earned them."

"I think it was around that time when my Dad showed up to my Career Day from my kindergarten class at Varsity View Community Center in Charleswood," recalls Brodie Bauer. "Most kids had their dads come in, some were in sales, some in construction, but I knew, nobody else's dad was going to top my Dad. When he came in dressed in full Blue Bomber gear, right down the helmet and pads, the kids went absolutely crazy. It was a complete frenzy. We all started screaming and my Dad gave a speech on what it was like to be a Blue Bomber. After that all the kids got up and tried to tackle him. It was incredible and all I could think was, I have the greatest Dad in the world."

Chapter Ten

But his retirement from the Winnipeg Blue Bombers wouldn't last. Those who knew him all had the same sense that #59, just couldn't stay away from the game.

"I knew he'd be back," said linemate, David Black. "Lyle had way too much passion and heart for the game to not be part of it."

"I remember him telling me that he and Heidi were going on a cruise with Cal and his wife," recalls Neal Fisher. "I had a feeling I was going to be in trouble and sure enough."

On February 21, 1992, just ten weeks after deciding to retire, the Winnipeg Blue Bombers introduced Lyle Bauer as their new assistant general manager.

"I had never given it much thought, but a GM position would be a great way to stay engaged in the game and make some changes I really felt needed to be done for the club and the players."

As the head coach, Cal Murphy had developed a special bond with Bauer that was evident both on and off the field. When Murphy moved from the sidelines to the front office, that relationship continued.

"Early on, Cal started sharing a lot more about the business of football," said Bauer. "He often asked me to attend and speak to sponsors and potential sponsors to help increase the team's revenues. I did quite a lot of that in the off season while working full time."

"I understood what went on in the locker room," said Bauer. "I knew those guys very well and in the off-season I had done business with a lot of them over the years in real estate."

"We used to bug Lyle all the time," said Walby. "We'd see him pushing Cal around in the wheelchair all the time. It was funny to watch, but we knew he was being groomed for that spot."

In early January, Darryl Rogers resigned as the Blue Bombers' head coach to take over the coaching duties for the Arkansas Miners of the Pro Spring Football League in the U.S. That left a hole in the coaching staff and speculation was that Cal Murphy wanted to get back to coaching, as well as keep his GM duties.

"After the year we had, I could see why Rogers wouldn't want to come back," said Bauer. "Things didn't fall into place for him or the team. The chemistry just wasn't there."

"I really wanted to help Cal and in order for him to have that dual role of coach/GM, he needed someone that had business acumen and understood the game both on and off the field," said Bauer. "It was definitely not about the money thing like some people assumed. Taking that position actually meant I was taking a 50% drop in my income compared to my playing and real estate salaries."

"I was up for the challenge. There were a lot of things in real estate that prepared me for the move. I believed that I understood business, and football is just another business. If you've got a good handle on the principles of management, you can always change commodities. I knew this wouldn't be any different if it were real estate, cars, or securities. We had a football team that we had to nurture and sell to the fans. And that's what I set out to do."

Bauer stepped into his new front office role with the same toughness and tenacity he had on the field. "I still had the urge to win. That never left me, but this playbook was quite different."

In 1991 the Winnipeg Football Club had lost $250,000 and was now in debt $1.1 million with outstanding contract guarantees of $1.9 million. Key veterans like Tom Burgess, Chris Walby, Nick Benjamin, Steve Rodehutskors and Rod Hill were unsigned going into the '92 season. Warren Hudson retired and Robert Mimbs' future with the team was up in the air.

"When he got to the front office he tried to re-do my contract," recalls Chris Walby. "I phoned him and he said, 'What do you want, Walls.' I told him this is what I want for cash and I want a riding lawn mower as a bonus. The next thing I hear is a dial tone. The bastard hung up on me. That's how hardcore he was. I mean, come on, we were roommates for ten years."

"Of course I remember that phone call," laughs Bauer. "Listen, the strategy always is to keep your opponent off balance. It worked on the field, so why wouldn't it work in the front office. Chris and I were close friends, brothers. I knew hanging up on him would really bother him more than if we had gotten into a heated argument. And it still bothers him after 25 years or he wouldn't still be talking about it."

Walby re-signed his contract in late March with the Winnipeg Blue Bombers.

"I had learned a lot from Cal," said Bauer. "Our relationship didn't really change from the time I was on the field. It just continued to grow. Obviously he had other responsibilities when he wasn't coaching, but you could tell he missed that part of the game. Cal was an on-field guy, but he loved the control he had with being the GM. I knew fairly early on that his objective was to do both if he could arrange it, so I understood my responsibilities."

Cal Murphy was known around the league for being frugal. He had a reputation as a tough, no nonsense negotiator when it came to contracts. "Whenever someone presented their first offer to him, his first response was usually 'Get real!'" said Bauer. "Followed by, 'You're not worth that.'"

"You never wanted to get into a contract dispute with him. You'd always lose out in the end," said Bauer. "In Cal's mind if you went into the last year of your contract and he couldn't sign you, he just assumed you were leaving anyway. He wouldn't put much effort into signing our own free agents. Ironically, he would sign other people's free agents."

"I remember Cal didn't offer me much," said quarterback, Tom Burgess, who led the team to victory in the 1990 Grey Cup game. "As I recall, he kind of low balled me a bit. I can't remember the exact amount, but it was similar to what I was making in 1991."

"Honestly, we never got into to any real negotiations," said Burgess. "I think he wanted to go in a different direction right from the start."

Enter Matt Dunigan, the gun slinging, free agent quarterback from the Toronto Argonauts. He had beaten the Blue Bombers on too many occasions while with the Toronto Argonauts and the B.C. Lions.

"Cal had his sights set on Dunigan," said Bauer. "Primarily because he knew was going to be the head coach. If Mike (Riley) had been the coach, Burgess would have still been there."

There were a couple of serious complications in the way if the team was to acquire Matt Dunigan. He was 31 years-old, badly beaten up with injuries and labeled a "Glass Quarterback." Mike McCarthy, the Argonaut's general manager suggested he was too old and their doctors weren't convinced he was worth taking a guaranteed gamble on. Dunigan had played in just 16 of 36 games and only finished 11 of them.

But the main issue with signing Dunigan was the money. He came with a high price tag. Dunigan wanted $500,000 guaranteed per season for two years. With the Blue Bombers' already in debt to the tune of $1.1 million, some felt the idea was too far-fetched when proven quarterback Tom Burgess was available for $200,000. But what Cal Murphy wanted, Cal Murphy got.

"The first thing we needed to do was make sure Matt was healthy enough to play," said Bauer. "And we needed to do that quietly. In April, I snuck him into Winnipeg without anyone knowing. We certainly didn't want the media finding out. Matt would have been easily recognized at the Winnipeg Airport, so we flew him into Grand Forks and I personally drove him across the border into Winnipeg. We had him checked out and cleared to play by our doctors."

"Once we got that green light, we set out to figure a way to financially secure him," said Bauer. That task would be daunting for the new assistant general manager.

The logical solution would have been a loan from the team's bank. Murphy tried, but was quickly declined. The next option was to approach the team's landlord, Winnipeg Enterprises Corporation with a deal. After several long closed door meetings, WEC agreed to front load a two year deal for Dunigan. But the Blue Bombers had to raise ticket prices by $2, $1 to the club and $1 to WEC. It was referred to as the Dunigan Tax. A $100,000 insurance policy was also put in place to indemnify the team in the case of a career ending injury to Dunigan.

"We got the deal done," said Bauer. "McCarthy was pissed at losing Dunigan, but all football guys are like that. They steal each other's players and then bitch when someone steals one of theirs."

"But overall, the deal made good business sense," said Bauer. "At that time, the average per cap concession was about $8 at a 35% net profit after paying the concessionaire. Over the course of a season, if we drew in an extra 50,000 in attendance, that would be $400k in additional revenue and net the team about $150k."

"Dunigan's billing was that of a star," said Burgess. "I was a solid player that played the role of pivot in relation to the supporting cast. I am not sure why Cal went in that direction, maybe he thought it would sell more tickets? Maybe he thought he needed that? I'm still not sure."

When the Dunigan deal was complete, there was little doubt Tom Burgess' career with the Blue Bombers had come to an end. But instead of worrying about the door that closed, Burgess considered the opportunities in the league that opened with Dunigan now off the market.

"I was a bit surprised he threw all that money at Dunigan, but I don't remember being all that upset. In my mind I was already thinking I was going elsewhere," said Burgess. "And in the end, Dan Rambo gave me a good deal in Ottawa, so it worked out fine."

With their new quarterback healthy and secured, Sam Garza and Danny McManus would be Dunigan's back-ups heading into the season. Steve Rodehutskors signed with the B.C. Lions and Tyrone Jones was dealt to the Saskatchewan Roughriders.

Bauer continued to establish himself in his new front office position by securing Labatts Manitoba Brewery as the clubs major sponsor for three years. The Blue Bombers and Labatts had a relationship for eleven years before a league move to Molsons in 1989. "That was a big deal for us. It took some of the pressure off."

After five years in the executive office, Cal Murphy was set to return to sidelines. In 1983, Murphy's first year with the Blue Bombers, the players had T-shirts made proudly displaying the fact that they had survived Camp Calsky. Going into the '92 training camp, there was little doubt that Murphy had mellowed. His coaching record with the Blue Bombers was 43-22-1. The man knew what he was doing.

But on June 2, Cal Murphy again admitted himself to the hospital after chest pains became too much to handle. In the short term, it was decided that Bauer would take over the GM duties, and offensive coordinator Urban Bowman, would step in as the team's head coach.

In the preseason, the Blue Bombers would go on to split their first two exhibition games. The first was a win against Saskatchewan, the second, a loss against Ottawa and their new quarterback, Tom Burgess.

In early July, Murphy's condition worsened and was marked as unstable. Some started questioning his future with the club. On July 11, Cal Murphy was flown to London, Ontario to wait for an assessment and possibly a heart transplant.

"Even in his condition, Cal absolutely wanted control of everything. I remember the day they were taking him on that life flight. He was barking out orders, telling everyone what to do. Cal was committed to his faith, his family and football, but some days it was hard for someone outside to know what order those came in."

"The club's President, Bruce Robinson and I visited him in London at the hospital and he would tell me what to tell Urban," recalls Bauer. "Little did we know that after we left that day, we almost lost him. They kept him alive for 24 hours before finally a miracle happened."

On July 15, during emergency by-pass surgery, a donor heart became available and Murphy underwent a heart transplant.

According to hospital officials, when he went on life support, he became the only heart transplant patient in the province to be rated a four on their four point priority system. The fact that a match became available so quickly had even the doctors at University Hospital a little bewildered.

Twelve hours after surgery, Murphy squeezed his wife's hand. His progress was encouraging, but it meant he would have to be away from his team for the rest of the season.

"He wasn't with us, but it was evident that this was still his team,'" said Bauer. "I was thrust into handling it all, but I was up for the challenge."

Seven days after his surgery, Murphy was frantically making phone calls demanding to know the score of the game between his Blue Bombers and Edmonton Eskimos.

For the next few weeks from his hospital room in London, Murphy spent as much time as the doctors would allow on the phone directing his team. Bauer would end up arriving at his London hospital room with a VCR and an armful of game tapes.

"When it was possible, we had the games on in his room," said Bauer. "We'd visit and develop game plans whenever we could."

"He was tenacious. He just wouldn't give up," said Bauer. "Cal was a real hard ass, but beneath that exterior he was kind, caring, and extremely generous. He reminded me a lot of my father."

Bauer settled in and ran the club with the same toughness and persistence he had learned from his mentor. He handled the team issues and had no problems taking on the league when called upon.

"When I took over as GM and made Urban Bowman the head coach, there was a power play. Urban didn't like Elfrid Payton as a defensive end, but I did. I told Urban that Elfrid was playing. Urban told me if that was the way it was going to be, I better have another coach ready to go. I told him that either he would be on the sidelines or someone else would be, it didn't matter to me. But Elfrid will be playing."

"I walked away after that not knowing if I had a head coach or not. Well, Urban gave in, Elfrid played and eventually became one of the most dominant defensive ends in CFL history."

On another occasion, midway through the season, Bauer was forced to stand his ground against the league office. In '92, the league expected visiting teams to arrive 24 hours before the game to allow local media access to the players. This would give them the opportunity to broadcast interviews during the local evening newscasts in the opposing city in the hopes of attracting higher ticket sales. But the Blue Bombers had booked tickets far in advance to take advantage of early booking discounts. Bauer refused to change the team's travel plans because of the cost involved and the league officials had no choice but to back down.

The CFL would take another financial blow when they would be forced to take over the B.C. Lions and use their television revenue to keep them afloat. In 1990, the Blue Bombers received $508,000 from the league. In 1991 they received just $130,000 due to $2.4 million spent to keep the Ottawa Rough Riders in business.

With the possibility of not receiving their share of the television revenue again, the financial pressure was building for the Blue Bombers. Bauer, again, approached the team's landlord for a deal. WEC eventually reduced the team's rent from $100,000 to $1 and approved a $1.5 million line of credit over three years.

"I was forced to learn some valuable lessons that first year," said Bauer. "One thing you have to realize is that the head coach, general manager and president/CEO all work with different agendas.

"Head coaches are only worried about the now and near future because they have to deliver or they're fired."

"General managers focus on the same, however there has to be some forward planning with things like personnel and finances."

"The CEO has to be concerned with all of that as well as the long term future of the team. Decisions made today impact the future."

"As an example, Cal had done several things as a coach that helped in the team in the short term, but were debilitating to the club for years to come. He had signed a long term radio deal with CJOB and got all of the money up front. I think it was $750,000. That money was spent immediately, but it still had to be accounted for during the entire term of the agreement. So the money was long gone, but we still had to show it as revenue in the team's future years."

In 1992, the Winnipeg Blue Bombers finished the regular season in 1st place in the East Division with an impressive record of 11–7 record. They would go on to beat Hamilton in the Eastern Final 59-11.

And nine months after retiring from an impressive 10 year career on the field, interim General Manager Lyle Bauer watched his team compete in the 80th Grey Cup at Toronto's Sky Dome Stadium. Cal Murphy had received permission from his doctors to join him, but all they could do was watch as the Blue Bombers went down in defeat against the Calgary Stampeders, 24-10.

"It was different," said Bauer. "Not being able to be there on the field with those guys was hard. But it was a difficult year for the team and the league as a whole. The toughest part for me was that there was a lot of old friends I played with that didn't make it through the '92 season. The cuts to guys like James Murphy and Perry Tuttle were difficult.

Back in Winnipeg and around the league, Bauer was being praised for the way he handled the 1992 season so it was no surprise when other doors started to open. Following their Grey Cup loss, rumours spread that Bauer was being courted as the possible GM to take over the B.C. Lions. "Yes, there was some talk of that floating around, but it didn't go anywhere," said Bauer. "Bill Comrie was the owner at the time and let's just say, we probably wouldn't have shared the same philosophies for the game on many levels."

"I was committed to Cal and the Blue Bombers. If I was going to have a GM or executive position, Winnipeg was where I wanted to be."

The following year, a healthy Cal Murphy resumed his GM and coaching duties with Bauer in the front office as the assistant GM. The team would again finish in 1st place in the Eastern Division with a 14–4 record. They appeared in the Grey Cup for the second straight year but lost to the Edmonton Eskimos.

1994 was the year of the disastrous CFL expansion into the U.S. That year the Winnipeg Blue Bombers finished in 1st place in the Eastern Division with a 13–5 record. They attempted to make a third straight Grey Cup appearance, but fell short against Baltimore in the East Final.

By May 1995, 13 years after arriving in Winnipeg to play on the line, Lyle Bauer made the shocking announcement that he was leaving the Winnipeg Blue Bombers and heading back to Saskatoon to take a management position with the Saskatchewan Wheat Pool and Agpro Grain.

"That was a difficult decision," said Bauer. "I loved Winnipeg and that team. Cal and I had grown even closer in those years."

But few people know, it was that close relationship between the two men that would become the reason for Bauer's departure from the team.

After the '94 season, several members of the Winnipeg Football Club's Board of Directors were quietly attempting to convince Bauer into assuming the general management position, leaving Murphy to the role of the team's head coach only.

"I couldn't do that to the man who had been such an influence on me and my career," said Bauer. "I learned everything from him, some good and I'll admit, some bad. But I owed him a lot."

"Cal had given me the chance to prove myself on and off the field when others didn't. He had taught me about priorities and loyalty. I watched his faith in action and how he just kept believing, no matter the odds. I like to think I lived that my entire life, but Cal Murphy truly reinforced that even more and in so many ways."

"I witnessed firsthand the lessons of how his faith, family and fight helped save his life. And I never would have imagined at the time that those same lessons probably saved mine."

Chapter Eleven

Between 1996 and 1999 the Blue Bombers posted a record of 29-61. Following the '96 season, Cal Murphy was fired after spending fourteen years with the Winnipeg Football Club.

"I didn't know Cal was being fired," said Bauer. "But I had heard rumours. We didn't have much contact after I had left until '97 when he was with Saskatchewan."

"I had to take a bit of a football break because it was so difficult to watch," said Bauer, recalling those years. "And it got even harder to watch when they were so bad on the field during the Reinbolt time. Jeff was a good guy but he was not prepared to be a head coach."

"I had to really be focused on the new business I was in. I did have corporate season tickets when I went to Calgary, but I let staff and customers use them. It was too difficult to just sit back and watch the game."

From '97 to '99 the roster of players and coaching staff for the Winnipeg Blue Bombers' never seemed to remain stable. It appeared to some that the team had lost its chemistry on the field and off. Season ticket sales plunged from a high of 17,000 in 1996 to less than 7500 in 1999.

Financially, the team was crippled by an accumulated debt of $5.4 million and the franchise was in grave danger of folding during the winter of 1999-2000.

"This was by far the worst period in Blue Bombers' history," said David Asper, who became formally involved with the team as a member of the Board in 1999. "The club was definitely in dire straits."

In December 1999, the Winnipeg Football Club's Board decided not to renew Ken Bishop's contract as the team's general manager. Several familiar names began circulating as Bishop's possible replacement.

"Truth be told," said Bauer, "I called Bob Miles, the president of the club to express my interest. I had been contacted quietly prior to that by several Bomber board members, representatives from Winnipeg Enterprises, the City of Winnipeg, and the province. But after speaking with Bob, the wheels went into motion very quickly."

On February 15, 2000, in what was the city's worst kept secret, the Winnipeg Blue Bombers called a press conference to introduce their new club President and CEO, Lyle Bauer.

After restructuring the way the club was being operated, the board of governors was abolished and Bauer was hired as a full-time, paid president with a Board of Directors.

"I think my reputation preceded me," laughs Bauer. "Joe Pop was quoted in Free Press, calling me a "street fighter with a business pedigree." I don't know if I would have taken it that far, but plain and simple, I couldn't stand to see what had happened to the club,"

"The staff members were advised that Lyle Bauer was the perfect fit because he had achieved success on and off the field and he understood both the player and business side of the Winnipeg Football Club," said Debra Lofvendahl, an administrative assistant with the club. "Right from the beginning I knew he was going to strive to make significant changes to bring financial stability to the organization. That was his main focus at the time, as the club was in financial debt."

"I think the key to me was the combination of business and football knowledge. I had a clear understanding of both and understood the balance between the two. Cal was primarily a football guy and Ken Bishop was a business man."

"I knew I could make a difference," said Bauer. "What I didn't know was how far it had fallen until I got in there. But there is one thing I have always said. Be careful what you ask me to do, because I will get it done, regardless of what gets in the way. I did it on the line against guys like Mike Walker, Bobby Thompson and Miles Gorrell."

"It took courage for him to come back," said Asper. "The organization was a mess."

"When I came back in 2000," said Bauer, "We still had to account for previous revenue, but we didn't have the benefit of the cash. It was all gone. It was very debilitating from an operational standpoint and the club's financial position was much worse than what was disclosed."

"We had to get the employees to bring their own toilet paper and office supplies. Some people said they didn't know if they even had jobs when they drove to work in the mornings," said Bauer.

"The club had taken $1million from their NFL development agreement in 1999 and put it all into revenue for that year to make that year's loss look less. That deal was for 5 years but they didn't account for it in that manner."

"Before I took the job the board was panicked about season tickets and did something really foolish," said Bauer. "They offered fans the opportunity to purchase season tickets at a discount. If a person agreed to purchase tickets for three years, they got a 10% discount the first year, 20% the second year and 30% the third year. They didn't even have to guarantee they would buy them after the first year. Even worse, the ticket prices were frozen at 1999 levels."

"That meant that every year our revenue would decline if we didn't sell more season tickets just to make up the difference. That program probably hurt us to tune of $1.5 million."

"Early on in that first season, I knew we were going to run out of cash and we desperately needed a loan. "I approached Hugh Campbell from the Edmonton Eskimos and he gave us a loan of $325,000 to keep us running," said Bauer. "Hugh and I had a great relationship and we were still great competitors. He had forgotten more about this business than I could ever learn."

"Next to Cal, Hugh has to be a man I admired the most and still do. He was so unassuming. He played the 'I'm just a football coach' act very well, but he was absolutely brilliant. He managed and maneuvered things the way he thought they should be but always in the best interests of the CFL first."

"When I was in management, I still wanted to win the Grey Cup as many times as possible," said Bauer. "The funny thing was, it wasn't important for me to win another Grey Cup because winning one in management could never have the same feeling as that of a player."

"I wanted to win them for the players; the Milton Stegalls, the Doug Browns, the Troy Westwoods, the Charles Roberts; all those guys that had played so hard, given so much but had yet to satisfied that insatiable desire to be a champion. Also for the fans, because they really are the backbone of that club and the CFL."

"When I first got in there, the support I received from the Alumni was amazing," said Bauer. "Particularly some of the older guys like Glen McWhinney, Ray Ash, Bill Todd, Kenny Ploen and others. These guys were at the Blue Bomber Stadium at night on the phones calling season ticket holders and asking them to renew. There was nothing in it for them except pride and knowing that they were helping the club."

"The previous management hadn't given the Alumni the respect they deserved. I was proud to bring them back into the fold and make them a part of the team. To this day, many make a point of thanking me for embracing them even though we were from different eras. I have and always will have great respect for them."

"I think the key from an organizational standpoint was to establish expectations. I made a pledge that we were no longer going to flounder. We were going to be successful on and off the field."

"The debt we had was like an anchor weighing us down, but the Blue Bombers' staff were committed to making things work. They just needed leadership."

"I cared about everyone in that organization, from the volunteers to the caretakers to the operations staff to the administration to the football operations. I knew them all by name and would make a point of speaking to them to find out things about them."

"They weren't the stars. They weren't in the limelight, but they were all believers and made sacrifices to make that club viable."

"He was certainly driven," said Gene Dunn. Dunn was appointed to the Blue Bombers Board by the City of Winnipeg in late 1999 and served as Vice-Chair in 2000. "Stubborn, but driven."

Heidi, Bauer's wife, had remained in Calgary for the first of the 2000 season. "We didn't want to move our daughter from high school when she was so close to graduating," recalls Heidi. "I knew Lyle was going to be working long hours. He's like that. When he gets focused, that's all he can think about. I think us staying behind really gave him the opportunity to make the changes he felt were necessary."

Bauer and the club's Board immediately set out to develop a strategic business plan that set out some lofty goals for the organization on and off the field. A stakeholders committee was established with representatives from the City of Winnipeg, the Province of Manitoba, the CFL and Winnipeg Enterprises.

"Trust me, we had some heated debates during those times," recalls David Asper. "Lyle's passion for team was always evident."

Once the business plan was completed, the club made the unprecedented move of releasing it to the media.

"We called it "2000 and Beyond." We released it to the media because we wanted our objectives to be out there and public. It held us accountable for the results to our stakeholders."

More importantly, it elevated the expectations of the club to the fans. When I got here, fans were saying 'All we want is to not be embarrassed anymore.' That is a disturbing statement. I came from a culture where winning was the only option and that was the expectation, period."

"Wrestling over the management of the stadium laid the foundation for financial security for the team. With control of the concessions, the operations and bringing stadium concerts and other events back to Winnipeg, we were able to secure the additional finances we needed to get out of debt and build a nest egg for the future."

"I remember we had $3.5 million in outstanding debentures that were coming due," said Gene Dunn. "The province had agreed to match those funds if we could get the debentures forgiven. Lyle set the way and got each one done. That impressed me. It really showed his knowledge of business and his commitment to the team."

"In regards to the debentures," said Bauer. "I met with almost each holder individually to get their support. It was a tough process because people thought 'here we go again.' I had to convince each one of them that this time it was going to be different."

"Have you ever looked at his eyes?" asked Dunn. "The look he gets when he loses is not something you ever want to see. I'm sure that helped when it came to straightening things out."

"We had trade payables in excess of $1.2 million. Some of them hadn't been paid for over a year. I personally made the commitment to each one of them they would be paid. By the end of the year, we paid off all of our trade creditors, 100 cents on the dollar."

From the moment he slid into the chair in his new office, things started to change. "It was important to change the way the business was being run," said Bauer. I was responsible for rebuilding the team and the day to day operations. The key, just like any other organization, is to put the right people in place to deliver in a variety of areas. "

Not only did Bauer have to tackle the team's financial woes, but the on-field situation for the Blue Bombers was just as troubling. He was taking over a team that had been a division doormat for three years with a record of 13-41 and they were close to losing key players like Kerwin Bell, Maurice Kelly, and Milt Stegall to free agency.

"I had the privilege of playing on those great teams with those great guys. People don't understand what it means to have that bond and that chemistry and that's important to building a winning team. I have always said that the feeling of winning a championship is the sharing of an indelible moment of time with your gridiron brothers and nothing can ever replace that. I knew what we needed to do to get us back to that point."

"There is a Harley Davidson slogan that kept coming up with me at that time: *'If I have to explain, you wouldn't understand.'* That is the same feeling one gets after winning multiple championships with a group of guys you would do anything for. And that's what we needed."

"People can think they know how to do it or know what it is like and what it takes, but they don't and never will until they earn that privilege and make that sacrifice."

The community support for the Blue Bombers was waning. The team had to sell 20,000 season tickets and raise $5 million in a short amount of time. "Winnipeggers want a winning team. They deserved it. Our community was there, but after a while, everybody loses interest in a losing team."

"My first 'introduction' if you want to call it that, to Lyle, was when I had to renew my contract," said Milt Stegall. "I had never met him personally, but we had a few conversations over the phone during the off season. He asked me to submit an offer. We did and his reply was 'You're not worth that.'"

"Milt was probably the hardest. I believe I told him he wasn't worth that much. I never did have much of a filter," Bauer laughed. But seriously, Milt and I got numerous deals done over the years and eventually we became good friends. He is definitely one of my all-time favorites, on and off the field."

"The one that got away, that still bothers me today was Arland Bruce. We couldn't out bid Toronto for him and he went there. That was a sore spot," recalls Bauer. "We offered more money than we had, but Toronto just kept going higher. That was the way it was going to be. Arland was a great talent but we had to move on. Our hands were tied due to finances and that was pretty much the story of my entire tenure in management."

Then there was Charles Roberts. In his 8-year playing career, Roberts had established himself as one of the premier running backs in the league, earning the nickname 'Blink' for his amazing quickness and agility.

"I am the reason Charles stayed in Winnipeg. Dave Ritchie didn't want him because of character reasons."

Off the field, Roberts struggled. He missed team flights and publicly criticized some of the decisions made by Head Coach, Dave Richie.

"I remember Charles quitting. I set up a meeting between him and I, and Lamar McRiggs, who was a good friend of his. We met at the Robins Donuts on Route 90 and I talked him into coming back. And, again, the rest is history." Bauer signed Roberts to a long term deal, against Ritchie's wishes.

"I don't think Dave ever accepted me as his boss," said Bauer. "He was a coach when I played, but now I demanded more from him than other people. He had gotten too comfortable after the team had experienced some success."

Bauer continued to put his stamp on the Blue Bombers throughout his tenure. "I knew what it was going to take and I was determined to do it."

In the 2000 season, Kerwin Bell was set to be the Bombers' starting quarterback. In the off-season they had acquired Khari Jones with the hopes that someday, he would take control of the team.

"I had watched Kerwin since he had been with Sacramento. He was a good quarterback, but I wasn't confident that he could get the job done. He was a pocket passer with no mobility."

By mid-August, seven games and just one victory in the 2000 season, Bauer made a bold move.

"We needed a shake-up. Khari was an up and comer that needed a chance. I called him into my office and said, 'I have one question for you. Are you ready to take this thing and run?' He said 'Yes.'"

"I took the chance. I cut Kerwin and made Khari the starter. I tried to trade Kerwin, but there was no interest from the other teams."

Not everyone was pleased with Bauer's decision. "I started getting death threats and was called a 'Nigger Lover.' But I was calm. I responded to one guy on the phone by telling him I was at the office, it was late at night and I would be more than happy to meet him out in the parking lot. Of course no one showed up."

In 1999, the Blue Bombers had finished in 4th place in the East division with a losing record of 6–12 and had failed to make the playoffs. In 2000, with Bauer positioned in the front office, the team finished in 3rd place in the East division with a 7–10–1 record. They appeared in the East Final playoffs for the first time in four years.

And by 2001, the Winnipeg Blue Bombers would finish in 1st place in the East division with a 14–4 record. They appeared in their first Grey Cup since 1993.

"I remember we were at the '01 Grey Cup in Montreal and Lyle and I were hosting a staff get together in the team room at the hotel," recalls David Asper who was Chairman of the Board at the time. "We were all having a great time and everyone was giving Lyle the gears about being the 'old man.' But Lyle kept insisting, 'I've still got some of it left.'"

"So, like an idiot, I said, 'Ok, let's see what it was like to line up against Lyle Bauer,'" Asper continued. "Everyone was laughing as him and I went into a three point stance in the middle of the room. We sort of played with each other, an arm up, a gentle swat, a nudge, then he said 'ready?'. I said 'Yes,' and then it was like getting hit by one of those machines that flattens cars!"

"David was technically my boss at the time," laughed Bauer. "And you don't hit your boss. But I looked over at

Gene (Dunn) and he just shrugged his shoulders and grinned. So I hit him."

"It was part one of a two part lesson I learned," said Asper. "Neither get hit by, nor drink with large current or past professional football players."

Taking a team to the Grey Cup is reason enough to celebrate, but the main focus has to be on playing the game at peak performance.

"Dave Ritchie really pissed me off at that Grey Cup," said Bauer. "Without my knowledge, he took the entire team to Less Browne's Grey Cup party the night before the game. Less was also on our coaching staff."

"It was the wrong message to send to our players before the game and it showed on the field the next day. Several players came in very late that night. I was absolutely furious. I told Dave it was bullshit and if he wanted to go to the Grey Cup as a spectator, he could go elsewhere."

The Blue Bombers would go down in defeat to the Calgary Stampeders 27-19.

But, despite the loss, Bauer had started rebuilding the team back to its former glory. The combination of Khari Jones, Milt Stegall and Charles Roberts brought the Bombers back to bringing the team back to their prominence, with Jones being the CFL's most outstanding player in 2001, and Stegall getting the honour in 2002.

"Some people said I made some ballsy moves back then," said Bauer. "But we made the playoffs that first year and returned to the Grey Cup in the second year."

"My most memorable Lyle Bauer moment during those years still makes me laugh," said Gene Dunn. "It was in 2002. We were standing on the sidelines with his son, Wesley, one day watching practice. The team had Mike Sellers on the roster at the time, a former Washington Redskins fullback. Mike was a beast; 6'4" and 275 pounds."

"Well, him and Lyle were nattering at each other. He's yelling at Lyle, telling him he's old and washed up. Then he came over and told Wesley to tell his dad to pay him more. Wesley said, 'The day you can take my Dad, then, maybe I'll tell him to pay you more.'"

"Later on, the three of us were walking through the tunnel and here comes Sellers again. Before I knew it, there was a thumping noise behind Wes and I. I turned around and saw Sellers on the ground with Lyle looming over him saying, 'Are we done now?'"

"I remember I rounded the corner in the stadium I saw Mike Sellers laying on the ground," recalls Wesley. "My father was stepping over top of him back towards the locker room with a big grin across his face. When I asked him what happened he said he wrestled Mike Sellers, took him to the ground and was going to continue on with his day."

From 2000 to 2004, the Winnipeg Blue Bombers would post a winning record of 51-38-1, making them one of the most dominant teams in the CFL. On the field, they were almost always favoured at home and away. Off the field, the financial future was looking bright.

"He was a pleasure to work with," recalls Bob Sokalski, the team's outside legal counsel. "Lyle had experience as a player, as a former player's rep and now as an executive. Whenever there was an issue that came up, he knew if it had merit or not. He had great knowledge of the entire game and the business."

"We were doing it," said Bauer. "We had increased our attendance every year. In 2000 we had reduced the 1999 loss by over a $1 million. After that we were profitable every year."

"Stubborn, tough and determined," recalls Gene Dunn.

Bauer was so tough, he brushed off the sore throat that started to develop in the summer of 2004. "It started to bother me in the summer and I thought it was just a sore throat. Nothing big. I took some antibiotics and thought that would take care of it."

"You have to understand that back in the 80's, Lyle and that group took great pride in their physical and mental toughness as well as their durability in not missing a game," said Ross Hodgkinson, who had been the Blue Bombers' head athletic trainer in the 80's, eventually becoming the team's assistant general manager under Bauer in 2002.

"Understanding the psyche of professional athletes and, in particular, offensive linemen is as much an art as it is science," said Hodgkinson. "Coaches often ask injured players if they can play. Few, if any will answer that question with a no. More often the response was, 'I think I can,' or 'I want to.'"

"The ability to distinguish between playing hurt and playing injured is paramount. Offensive linemen, because of their physical and mental toughness, combined with the nature of that position could play with a significant amount of pain. Lyle was certainly no exception to that rule."

"Lyle may have been one of the most stubborn of that collective group that didn't want to be seen in a training room. Case in point was him removing the cast on his leg in 1984. We are taking about a group that took great pride in their physical and mental toughness and refused to miss a game."

"The best way to explain to a player whether he should play or not, was simply ask him this question? "What is the difference between an injured player and a bad player?" The answer is simple, "Nothing, they both look like shit.' No player wants to go out and embarrass himself or hurt the team."

But when the first course of antibiotics didn't help, the old lineman still ignored it, because he didn't want to miss a game. Any game.

FOR IMMEDIATE RELEASE
December 14, 2004
From the desk of Lyle Bauer, President, Winnipeg Football Club

Winnipeg, MB - As the Winnipeg Football Club prepares to celebrate its 75th anniversary, it will also mark the 20th year of my association with this proud franchise.

Personally, this year will present a significant challenge for my family and myself. Most recently I have been diagnosed with a malignant orpharyngeal tumour for which we will begin treatment immediately. These treatments will occur over the next number of months.

As discussed with the board of the WFC, it is my intention to continue as the president/CEO, aided by the strong management team and staff. The management team assembled here is no accident. They are highly skilled in their respective areas of expertise. Succession planning is paramount for sustainable success.

The WFC has a solid business plan for the future with specific goals and objectives both on and off the field. We as a team, an organization, and community, have come too far not to succeed.

I would like to thank the support that I have received from the board and specifically chairman Gene Dunn, past chair David Asper and vice-chair Ken Hildahl. Also, special thanks to Ross Hodgkinson, who has helped me on some dark days. My family and I are forever grateful to all of you.

This will be a new and significant challenge and I would like to thank my new team, the staff and medical providers at CancerCare Manitoba.

To those who have walked this path before me, I owe a great deal of gratitude for their experience and strength.

This development comes with much surprise as I have been told that I do not fit the profile or lifestyle for what I have contracted. This in itself should send a clear message to thousands of people out there today. Early detections, treatment and research as the keys to a future world where "all cancers can be beaten."

Thank you for your support.

Lyle and Heidi Bauer and family

Chapter Thirteen

"I hate doctors, not personally. I just didn't like the process. If you have to see a doctor, it means you have something wrong with you and that's something I could never admit."

"It was just a sore throat that wouldn't go away," said Bauer. "I finally went to see John Peterson. He was one of the team doctors we had when I played. I trusted John."

"Back In the 80's I remember tearing my bicep muscle," recalls Bauer. "Surgery they said. Screw that. Not me. I wasn't going for surgery. It would have meant missing games and there's no way was going to do that. So I continued playing in a lot of pain instead of letting my team down."

"So a sore throat wasn't going to stop me. I had a team to run. The staff, the players, the community, they were all counting on me. I figured antibiotics would get rid of it."

But the antibiotics didn't help and Bauer let it drag on for another few weeks before contacting Peterson again. "He referred me to Dr. Donna Sutherland, an ear, nose, and throat specialist at the Health Sciences Center."

"Even then they still couldn't find anything after doing several more tests, but it continued to bother me. John called Doctor Sutherland again and told her there was something wrong. He told her it was really bothering me."

More tests and a scan finally revealed that there was definitely something there. "That's when I was told that cancer was a possibility. They mentioned another test, but I didn't really hear it."

"Lyle's biggest concern was what he was going to tell Heidi and the kids," said Gene Dunn. "I was in his office when he found out, but it still wasn't confirmed. There was another test coming, but I think he knew. He never once mentioned dying. He wasn't concerned about his own life. His wife and children were first and foremost the entire time."

"I don't think I have ever felt so alone in all my life," said Bauer. "Thoughts, fears, concerns, they all come crashing in and there's nothing you can do about it."

"For years I battled some of the biggest bad asses in football because I wanted to. But I watched game film to alleviate those risks. I'd spend hours studying my opponent so I could gain even the slightest advantage over them," said Bauer, with a look of anger in his eyes. Gene Dunn had previously mentioned the look of Bauer's eyes when he got angry. "I saw that look many times after a loss. It's not something you ever want to witness," said Dunn.

"When I took the assistant general manager position, it was my choice. Stepping into the CEO office against some unfavourable odds was again, my choice, but still, something I was prepared for. But this? Hell, no! I didn't ask for this!"

The next test, called a panendoscopy, was quickly scheduled at the Health Sciences Centre. A panendoscopy is the diagnostic procedure doctors used to examine Bauer's throat, larynx, esophagus, windpipe, and bronchi. The procedure looked for visible signs of a tumor and allowed doctors to use a special instrument through the scope to biopsy pieces of tissue that looked potentially cancerous.

"They had to shove a tube down my throat so I could breathe," said Bauer. "That was horrible because I had to be awake, but after that I was put right out."

"The wait was horrible," said Heidi who had accompanied her husband. "I didn't want to be there. I just wanted to go home."

While recovering from the panendoscopy in the post op room, Heidi, nervously sat by her husband's bedside. "When he started to wake up and I told him to grab his clothes and get dressed so we could leave. I didn't want to know. I didn't want to be there," she recalls.

But before they could leave, Dr. Sutherland entered the room holding a clipboard.

Throat cancer, Stage 4. Just hearing the word cancer can have a profound effect on even the strongest person. The exact medical term for Bauer's diagnosis was oropharyngeal cancer, a disease in which malignant cells had formed in the tissue of oropharynx. The oropharynx is the middle part of the throat that includes the base of the tongue, the tonsils, the soft palate, and the walls of the pharynx.

The psychological effects of hearing a cancer diagnosis are often similar to those of grief. Shock, denial, anger, bargaining, depression and acceptance can all be part of the same framework. But with a cancer diagnosis, learning to live with the fear of an uncertain future is added to the mix.

It's important to understand that the emotional stages that can develop after a cancer diagnosis are not necessarily in any set order and there isn't a specific timeline. There also isn't a set progression from one stage to the next. In reality, any one of the different stages can come at any time or they could all hit at the same time. The only thing that is certain about a cancer diagnosis is that it's going to hit and it's going to hit hard.

"To this day, I couldn't tell you exactly what Dr. Sutherland told us," said Bauer. "But I do know, it was a punch in the face that put me in a fog for the next few days. I was in shock. Nothing made sense. For ten years I had taken brutal, vicious hits in the field, but nothing like this."

"Let's go. Let's get out of here," Heidi remembers saying. "That was my first and only thought. I didn't want to stay. I wanted to take my husband and go home. I didn't even want to know. I wasn't ready to face the reality of it."

"The ride home was an absolute fog," said Bauer trying to recall the ride back to their Stonewall home. "I was still feeling the effects from all the anesthetic drugs they had given me and the shock of the whole thing. But I do remember that not a single word was spoken."

"When we got home, Heidi and I both sat in the living room in a daze for what seemed like days. There are bits and pieces that come and go, but I couldn't tell you exactly what happened and when."

"When Lyle and I first got together, I remember him saying he was going to play football," said Heidi. "Okay, I said. I was young. I didn't know better. We had always worried about the future, but we felt the future would somehow look after itself."

"I had always planned for the future," said Lyle. "But not this. What was going to happen to my family if I was gone? What do I tell the kids? How do I tell the kids?"

"I'll never forget that day," said Wesley, Bauer's oldest son. "I had just finished a long day of exams at St. Paul's High School. I walked out, relieved that the exams were behind me and I could just relax."

"I opened the truck door and immediately caught my Dad's eyes. They were completely red and were all welled up. This was the first time I had ever seen my Dad this way and immediately I was concerned. We started to drive home and he told me that he had been diagnosed with cancer. Right away, I flipped my head to the window and started to break down crying. I didn't know what to say. I just grabbed his hand and we stayed silent the entire way home."

"As a 16 year old boy who had spent every second idolizing his father and what he had done for his family, I truly could not find the words."

"I was working at the office when all this was happening," said daughter, Danni. "I knew something was up."

"My Dad in my mind was invincible," said Brodie, Bauer's son. "He was the strongest man I'd ever known, both physically and mentally. So to hear that he was diagnosed with stage 4 cancer was a shock to say the least."

"That whole week, my hands were shaking, my heart pounded and the only word I heard inside my head was 'cancer,'" said Bauer. "I began to experience depths of fear and confusion that I'd never known before."

"For the first in my life I had no control over something. So how do I control not having control? How do I do this? How do I not lose control of the control I don't have. In my head I kept repeating, 'I want to grow old with my wife. I want to watch my kids grow up.'"

Halfway across the city, far from Winnipeg Stadium, a different type of team was forming and putting a game plan together. "We had to gather his treatment team pretty quickly," said Dr. James Butler, Chair of the Head and Neck Disease Site Group at CancerCare Manitoba and the attending radiation oncologist.

Having grown up in East St. Paul, Butler was familiar with his patient from his playing days. "Of course I knew who Lyle Bauer was," said Butler. "Who doesn't? I grew up watching the guy play."

"Over the years, I've had many high profile patients, but regardless of who the patient is, the process is still the same. The first step is assembling the entire treatment team into the amphitheater. There, we meet the patient, and as a team, we analyse the test results and the records. Then we develop a detailed treatment plan."

"That session was scheduled for the following week," recalls Bauer. "I was still in that fog where nothing made any sense. I remember getting ready to leave for the appointment, but all I could think about was the garbage. It was garbage day and it had to be taken out, but I forgot. Heidi, Wes and I were in the truck and all I could focus on was going back and taking the damn garbage out. I turned the truck without really thinking around and we ended up in the ditch. My anger took over and I floored it to try and get out. We hit the other side of the ditch even harder. Heidi thought we were going to flip."

"We managed to get the truck out," said Wesley. "Dad just said, 'I have a lot on my mind.' I would say that was the only time I saw my father affected by his diagnosis."

"I did get us to the appointment in one piece," said Bauer. "Heidi and I walked in and were taken to the amphitheater. There were about thirty people in the room, but I don't remember seeing anyone. I was led up on a stage and Heidi was shown to a seat off to the side."

"They started examining me on the stage and posting images up on a big screen. My mind wasn't focused, but I recall they were all taking notes and talking about something. I was in the room, but I wasn't present."

"Eventually, I was led off the stage, barely able to hold myself together. Heidi and I went to a room somewhere in the clinic where we waited for I think about an hour. I'm usually never at a loss for words, but this was different," said Bauer.

"Then one by one, the oncologists came in. First it was Dr. Donna Sutherland, who had done the panendoscopy. She informed us of what was coming. She explained that in my case, surgery was not an option as it would cause far too much damage. I would lose most of my tongue. Their plan was to use an aggressive combination of radiation and chemotherapy treatments. It was difficult to comprehend at the time."

"Next it was Dr. Andrew Maksymiuk, who explained that chemotherapy was going to be used to enhance the effects of the radiation. Their plan was to take me as far as I could go physically to kill the cancer and then bring me back. I remember Andrew had a very calm methodical approach in his discussions."

"Then Jim Butler came in the room," said Bauer. "He came in hell bent for action and I could tell this was no game for him."

After graduating with an International Baccalaureate Diploma from Miles MacDonell Collegiate, Jim Butler attended the University of Winnipeg and received a BA in History before entering medical school.

In 1994, Dr. Butler was granted a MD, CM degree from McGill University and starting training in radiation oncology at both McGill and the University of Manitoba. He received his FRCPC designation in 1999, and undertook fellowship training in conformal radiotherapy at the University of Michigan.

He returned to Winnipeg in 2000, at almost the same time Bauer had assumed the role of the Blue Bombers' CEO and coordinates the local Fellowship Program in Radiation Oncology.

Dr. Butler has chaired the Head & Neck Disease Site Group at CancerCare Manitoba since 2004, and sits on several administrative / technical committees at CancerCare Manitoba. He is also an Assistant Professor at the University of Manitoba. He and his colleagues were honoured with the Innovative Team of the Year Award in 2008 for their work in developing intensity modulated radiation therapy treatments at CancerCare Manitoba.

"I don't think Heidi was too impressed with him at the time. But I realized Jim was the 'James West' of radiation oncologists. He was focused and determined to win, because to him, losing wasn't an option. He was intense and intimidating, but committed to saving my life."

"Jim knew we were thinking of going to the Mayo Clinic. He told us that was fine, but that we couldn't wait too long, because this thing wasn't going to wait for us. The clock was ticking."

"We made the decision to stay and after that we went into a whole series of planning stages, casting for the mask, blood work, tattooing for the radiation targeting, meetings with dietitians and other support services. It was a whirlwind," said Bauer.

"Chemotherapy was starting immediately. Basically they told me, 'We're going to poison you and torture you for next few weeks in the hopes of saving your life. It might not work, but we have to start now.'"

As the first intravenous needle was being inserted into Bauer's arm, news spread throughout Winnipeg and the football community quickly. Blue Bombers Chair, Gene Dunn, assembled the team's executive staff together in the boardroom to inform them of the situation.

"The staff gathered and we were told the news that Lyle was diagnosed with throat cancer," said Debra Lofvendahl, Bauer's Executive Assistant at the time. "I swallowed my heart, trying to fight back my tears. It was devastating news that none of us expected to hear. We all sat silent, staring at each other in shock and disbelief."

"It was a complete shock," said Ross Hodgkinson, who was now the team's assistant general manager. "Lyle had no real factors that would give an indication he would be predisposed to throat cancer. He was very fortunate to have access to an outstanding group of medical practitioners through the club. In particular Dr. John Peterson, who knowing Lyle's toughness and ability to play with pain insisted on persevering with tests when the initial tests were negative."

"When I first heard it, I was numb," said Chris Walby. "We had lost so many; so many good ones. Then I find out this and think "Not another one. This was my brother. You start to question your own mortality. Back in the day, I wasn't scared of shit, but this? It doesn't matter how tough you are, we're all vulnerable."

"Devasted," said David Black when he heard the news. "We were close, brothers. Lyle and I had a special relationship during our playing days and that bond grew stronger over time. I would have done anything for him."

While the Blue Bombers' staff sat quietly in shock, the team released the Bauer's press statement to the public. "That was Lyle's idea," said Heidi. "I didn't agree with him. I didn't want it made public. I figured we could deal with it just us, him and I together. But Lyle wanted everyone to know because he knew there would be others, and maybe through all this, he could find some way to help someone else."

"I now know what it's like to lie in bed at night and wonder," What's going to happen?" I saw how it was affecting Heidi. My job was to love and protect her and she didn't deserve to go through this. Neither did my kids. Do what you want to me, but don't ever mess with my family. The fear and anxiety just kept building and I realized the worst thing you can do with fear and anxiety is to ignore them and pretend you're strong."

"There had to be a shift and it was going to come from me. It started after the treatment meeting we had with the medical team. I was starting to develop confidence from them and I knew I had to let them do their work. It was time for me to shut the fuck up and do my job, which came down to letting them do theirs."

"I had to be strong both mentally and physically. I started gathering information, just like I used to do in my playing days. But instead of game film, I contacted others who had gone down the same road I was about to travel. I learned everything I could possibly learn about this disease and the treatment."

"I don't lose well. I never have," said Bauer. "I've learned that the sting of a loss stays with me longer than the joy of victory. There are games I lost in high school that still bother me. I hate the taste of a loss."

"It was time for me to just put my head down and get ready for the fight of my life. I had my medical team and my support team with me."

"I drew strength from all of them and my memories of Cal Murphy. His tenaciousness and his faith had stayed with me for a reason," said Lyle. "I've always felt I had faith and maybe it was something I took for granted in the past. I never knew how to lean into it. But Heidi's family was strong in their faith and they showed me what faith can do. I found comfort in them. I felt their prayers and the prayers from all the others. I found myself praying before every appointment, treatment, MRI, and scan for the strength to continue the fight."

"Our relationship kind of went sour after a bad contract negotiation and we hadn't spoken in quite a while," said James West. "But when I heard, I called him immediately. I prayed for him as hard as I could."

"In one of our earlier appointments," said Bauer. "Dr. Butler suggested that I would need to have a feeding tube inserted. Nourishment was going to be critical, but my neck, mouth and throat were going to be too sore from the burning of the radiation to continue eating normally. I got on the phone and started talking to people who had been down this road before. Some had the feeding tube while others didn't. I weighed the pros and cons. My fear was that I may lose the use of my facial muscles from lack of use. I took the chance and decided not to have the feeding tube."

"One of my techs told me about Lyle's decision with regard to the feeding tube," said Dr. Butler. 'He told me that Lyle was afraid to tell me. He didn't want to upset me. But this was his treatment. He was the one in control. It's something we try and stress to all our patients. They have to take ownership in the process and he was definitely doing that."

"His determination and toughness carried him through and contributed to his treatment with cancer," said Ross. "Lyle barely missed a beat at work while enduring unprecedented levels of radiation treatment. I remember seeing him in the coach's locker room during his treatment and his neck looked like someone had taken a blow torch to it."

"He never once complained," said Brodie "He took it day by day. Some days where obviously worse than others, but even in his worst moments he'd be able to knock off a few good one liners. Most people would be forced to take time off of work, but not my Dad. Even while fighting cancer my Dad would be at the Bomber office putting in full days. He truly bled Blue and Gold."

"That 'win at all cost' attitude is what he took into his cancer battle," said Walby. "The 'I'm better than you' had been ingrained in him for years. "'I will not be defeated. I've fought the tough battles.'"

"We all played with injuries back then," Walby continued. " That's the way it was. To Lyle, this was just another battle. It was a bigger battle and I have no doubt there was fear. But we had been taught not to show fear. You swallow it. You beat it. You don't give one inch. On the field, if you show fear, you're dead. Your opponent can smell it on you. I know he said 'Mr. C, now you're in for the battle of your life.' Cancer definitely picked the wrong guy to mess with this time."

Forty-two radiation treatments, sometimes three times a day, started in January 2005. "Everyone literally associated with the Blue Bombers were all committed to support Lyle and his family anyway we could," said Debra.

"Lyle would disappear for a lengthy time period while he was going through the chemo and radiation treatments," said Debra. "When he returned to the office, he was frail, but determined to be back even though he was extremely weak. He's a very strong and determined individual and was very committed to the organization."

"I chuckle now a little thinking back when he would rest after his treatments," she said. "Lyle had a couch in his office and he would let me know when he was going to lie down and rest. I took that to mean I was to trade in my assistant's hat for a Pitbull collar. I was tenacious! I sat right outside his door and if anyone approached, I firmly told them to 'step away from the door.' Under no circumstances was he going to be disturbed."

"I remember seeing him at a function," said Walby. "I hugged him but it felt like there was nothing there. He wasn't the same guy. Half of him was gone."

"He never let it affect my life or childhood which says a lot," recalls Wesley. "He was still at every volleyball game I played. He made sure that he was present at every major event as I grew up. Now that I looked back it is incredibly remarkable, because I know how ill he felt."

"The only comfort I could take was knowing my Dad had always been a warrior," said Brodie Bauer. "Nothing was ever handed to him. He had earned his living battling and I knew that's exactly what he was going to do with his fight against cancer."

"I'm not going to lie," said Bauer. "It is not an easy thing to find out you've got cancer and that you could possibly die. The truth is we're all going to die someday, but to have a doctor sit across from you and tell you there's a possibility of that happening in the near future... it shakes you up."

"Here's the thing about cancer, you're all alone in it. It doesn't matter who else is there. In an instant, I was taken to a place where everybody else was okay except me. Heidi, who is undeniably committed to me, held my hand, and we wept together. My brothers, Chris, Blackie, West, Gene, Ross, Debra and so many others, came alongside my family and held me up with their support. People from all over the city, the country and the league encouraged us. People came over just to sit in my house and my office to pray with me and for me."

"But all that doesn't change the fact that at night, when everybody went to sleep, it was just me laying there, staring at the ceiling and wondering am I going to be here when all of this is over? If my eyes were to close because of death, what would happen next?"

"Leading up to that treatment meeting, if I looked into the eyes of my wife or one of my children, it was a fight to hold myself together. But I discovered that inside all the fear and anxiety, behind all the tears, there was a quiet confidence that was starting to build up inside of me. In the days and months to come, my entire world was about to sink in, but because of the love and support around me, I found my footing and was able to take one step at a time."

"If you were to ask people about me today, depending on who they are, they may tell you I am a Grey Cup Champion, or a CEO. But in reality, I'm also a husband, a father, a son and a friend. And here's the truth that slammed into me in December 2004. One day I may not be running a football team. I may not be Heidi's husband or my kids' father. There was a chance I would never get to laugh at one of Walby's stupid jokes ever again. All those things that truly define who I am could be gone and that still scares me today. The thought of dying can bring an uncanny clarity to one's life."

"A cancer scare can make one come to terms with who they really are and what they have. When the fog clears, you get a picture of what to hold on to and what to let go. Today, as I look around, I notice my wife grows more beautiful by the hour and my children bring me a new found glory that is beyond words. My three Grey Cup rings don't quite look the same anymore, but the memories of my brothers that come from winning those rings increase in value every time I look at them."

"There were times in my life when I believed I was tough enough and smart enough to handle anything. But I have grown exponentially since that day in December 2004. This journey not only changed me as a man outwardly, but more significantly, as a man inwardly. It's not that my behaviour has changed, but rather the desires of my heart have been modified. I didn't use to think like this before. I always thought it was my strength and toughness, but I was wrong. Dead wrong. Now I hope when I do go and I'm done with this game, I would be remembered not just as a Grey Cup Champion, but as a faithful husband, a loving father and a close friend."

Chapter Fourteen

Even before his last treatment was completed, Lyle Bauer had a vision for the Never Alone Foundation already set up in his mind. His vision was simple; to create a world where no one enters the fight against cancer feeling alone.

"It was important to me that people know there's a support mechanism out there," said Bauer. "People shouldn't have to feel alone in their fight."

"Throughout my fight, I was deeply touched by the support of so many and made a commitment to pay it forward by helping others. I still am when I think about it. I feel like it's part of the debt I now owe."

"There's a story I like to tell," said Heidi when she recalls those early days of her husband's battle. Humour can sometimes bring light to those dark moments that sometimes refuse to leave.

"For two months, due to the radiation treatments, Lyle couldn't speak. It was hard for him because of the pain he was in. He would save his voice for the work he had to do, because he was still committed to the team." There are numerous accounts and comments of how Bauer rarely missed a day at the Blue Bombers' office.

"Our first Never Alone function was actually going to take place at the CFL Coach of the Year Awards Luncheon," said Heidi. "I knew I was going to have to speak in front of 500 CFL officials. I'm a very private person and I was extremely nervous about having to speak in front of all those people."

"I went out and bought a new leather skirt. I guess I thought it would make me feel more confident," she said.

"Lyle and I got up in silence that morning. The entire time we were getting ready, there was no conversation. I got dressed and was really quite happy with the way I looked," she said. "I walked over to him, looking for a nod of approval."

"He looked at me and spoke the first words I'd heard in weeks from my loving husband, "That is the ugliest skirt I've ever seen."

Bauer did not speak at the January luncheon, but his presence in the room was enough to say it all.

The Coach of the Year Award was presented to Greg Marshall, the Hamilton Tiger-Cats' rookie coach, but he wasn't the real winner of the day. The Winnipeg Blue Bombers handed over the entire proceeds from the luncheon, a $25,000 cheque to the CancerCare Foundation. His vision for the Foundation was becoming a reality.

"His recovery was really a miracle when you think about it," said Debra. "We were never told at the time that Lyle's diagnosis was Stage 4. His courage and strength to survive was not just for himself and his family in the end, but to help others going through the same fight to never feel alone."

"It was around that time I went back to working out religiously," said Bauer. "I was still in the game, a starter and it was my way of keeping up my strength. It seemed like I was fighting battles on a couple of different fronts."

In mid-April, 2005, Bauer stood behind the podium in the team's press room, and in front of the media, in a voice barely audible, reported that the Winnipeg Blue Bombers had posted a profit for the 2004 season of $75,041. It was a modest amount by most standards, but it was a key indication that the team had turned a corner. The health of the Winnipeg Blue Bombers and their CEO was improving. Bauer's radiation treatments were finished and the team's $5.4 million dollar debt was shrinking.

Bauer's report highlighted the team's four straight years in the black. The team was almost debt free and looking forward to reaping the benefits of hosting the 2006 Grey Cup. It was a dramatic turnaround for a community-owned franchise that had once been on the brink of bankruptcy.

But the healthy financial results weren't translating to the team's record on the field. In 2004, the Winnipeg Blue Bombers had finished in 4th place in the West division with a 7–11 record. The team had failed to make the playoffs for the first time since 1999.

Longtime quarterback and face of the team, Khari Jones, had been traded in 2004. "Khari's arm was not good and he struggled to make certain throws," said Bauer. "It was actually his shoulder. That was a tough one, as I really like Khari and his wife, Justine. He was good for the club and for Winnipeg, but it had to be done."

"I consider not making the playoffs to be a poor season. I always have. It's just not acceptable," said Bauer. "Quite frankly in '04, our Head Coach, Dave Richie had started to lose interest in the team and his health was a concern."

"I knew he had a heart condition that required attention. I offered Dave a long term contract in April, but he wouldn't agree to it so he went into the '04 season with a level of uncertainty."

"My dilemma was having a coach with a heart issue and a team that was struggling," said Bauer. "To make matters worse, I knew that Dave wouldn't have health coverage after the season if he was to have heart surgery."

"When we got off to a bad start, I knew the board wouldn't approve a new contract for Richie at the end of the year. After we got our asses kicked on a Western swing, I had several calls from the board executive."

"So I made a difficult decision. I let Dave go knowing it wouldn't be a popular decision but it would be best for the club in the long term," said Bauer. "More importantly, it was better for Dave and his wife Sharon."

"Within weeks of letting Dave go, he had heart surgery so I know I had made the right decision," said Bauer. Dave and Sharon both hated me for it, but I knew it was the right thing to do."

"I was working at the box office at the time," said Danni, Bauer's daughter. "I remember some people were pretty pissed off over Dave Richie's dismissal. We were doing season ticket renewals and someone faxed in their renewal with a letter saying 'Hey Lyle Bauer, your cancer is karma for letting Coach Richie go. Hope it gets you in the end."

"A few years later, I had the opportunity to see Sharon at a Grey Cup game," said Bauer. "I told her that I knew they hated me, but that decision may very well have saved Dave's life. After that we started some reconciliation, however, I am sure there is still some resentment there. Going through what I did with Cal, I didn't want to do it again. I was very concerned that Dave would have a heart attack on the field."

"I feel bad about that, because I really liked them, but sometimes you have to do the tough things in life."

"Jim Daley wasn't the best option as a head coach, but deserved to continue since he picked up when we let Dave go."

In 2005, the team finished in 5th place in the West division with a 5–13 record and again failed to make a playoff appearance.

"The Ottawa Renegades team suspended operations just before the 2006 season," said Bauer. "The league wanted us to move back to East division. I wasn't happy with that and made my opinion known."

"He negotiated an extra $700,000 from the league," said Gene Dunn. "I was shocked when they agreed to it. That was all Lyle."

"In 2006, we hired Doug Berry as head coach and had a 9-9 season and made the playoffs," said Bauer. "That isn't a losing season."

Quarterback Kevin Glenn, along with Milt Stegall and Charles Roberts led the Bombers back to respectability in 2006. The season included many highlights, but none as exciting at what became known as 'The Play' on July 20, 2006.

Trailing the Edmonton Eskimos on the road 22–19, and facing third and long on their own 10-yard line with 4 seconds left in the game, Milt Stegall caught a 100-yard TD pass from Kevin Glenn as time expired to win the game 25–22. It is considered by many as the greatest play in CFL history.

The Blue Bombers ended up making their first playoff appearance in two years. Despite losing in the first round, optimism going into the 2007 was higher than ever.

The 2007 CFL season was in some ways the year of Milt Stegall. Stegall broke the career CFL touchdown record, but fell just short of overtaking the career receiving yards record held by Allen Pitts.

The 2007 Grey Cup game was played between the Winnipeg Blue Bombers and the Saskatchewan Roughriders, the first time the two prairie teams met for the championship. During the East division final win over the Toronto Argonauts, Blue Bombers' quarterback Kevin Glenn broke his arm leaving inexperienced rookie Ryan Dinwiddle to take his place for the championship game.

Dinwiddie, in his first CFL start, managed to throw just one touchdown pass, but fumbled once and threw three interceptions. The Blue Bombers were defeated by the Saskatchewan Roughriders 23–19.

In January, Bauer signed Milt Stegall to a one-year contract for $200,000. Stegall took a $50,000 pay cut, but knew the Blue Bombers were a contender to win the Grey Cup that year. He started the season 159 yards away from breaking Allen Pitts' all-time receiving yards record.

The Winnipeg Blue Bombers again made a run at the Grey Cup, but lost in the Eastern Semi-Final game against the Edmonton Eskimos, who had crossed over from the West.

On November 12, Head Coach, Doug Berry was relieved of his duties with the club.

A month later, the Blue Bombers announced Mike Kelly would lead the team into the 2009 season as their head coach. The return of Kelly opened a new Cal Murphy era, and the board hoped to bring back Murphy's success.

"I first met Lyle in early March of 1992," said Kelly. "He had just finished his playing career the previous year and Cal Murphy immediately took him on as Assistant GM. I came in a few months later when Cal made the decision to return to the sidelines as Head Coach and he initially hired me as the receiver's coach."

"That first season was when Cal had a heart attack that required a transplant," said Kelly. "That thrust Lyle into a leadership role as the interim GM. Half way through the season I was named Offensive Coordinator. Lyle and I bonded very well. We both took on added responsibilities, in essence getting thrown from the frying pan into the fire."

"But it was a special time and we ended up in the 80th Grey Cup as Eastern Division Champions. His no nonsense and straight forward leadership style fit well with my own beliefs," said Kelly.

"When he hired me in early December of 2008 as the Head Coach, I was extremely excited to work directly with him again. We had remained friends for all those years and he visited me in Orlando when I was with the XFL and in Philadelphia when I was in the NFL."

"We ate breakfast nearly every morning in 2009 at 6:00am, rarely wavering from the same orders from Tim Horton's," recalls Kelly. "It gave us an opportunity to address all aspects of the football club and there were never any elephants in the room because Lyle will speak his mind and look for solutions."

After his hiring of Mike Kelly, things stated to turn in the organization. "There was some strain at the board level," said Bauer. "I had come back to a situation with an insurmountable debt and poor performance, on and off the field. We resurrected the club and had well in excess of $5.5mm in the bank with no outstanding debt."

"When the club was in dire straits and beyond bankruptcy, the board wanted nothing to do with the team, on or off field," said Bauer. "All they would say was 'Just fix it.'"

"But once we got some credibility, all of a sudden some board members believed it was them that did it and that they knew everything about the football business.

"When I wanted to hire the best of the best for a head coach, we were always told to look at people who were out of work or inexperienced at the position," said Bauer. "Not that those people don't deserve the opportunity, but it takes time. Case in point, just look at the team's situation today."

"Being told I couldn't use some of the funds to improve our on field product... that didn't sit well. As you have come to know, I have certain principles and beliefs that are etched in stone. I wanted to win a Grey Cup for our fans. We had been to the cup twice and lost. And we did it on a shoe string budget."

The team would go on to finish the '09 season with a disappointing 7–11 record. They had been in playoff contention until the last game of the season, at home against the Hamilton Tiger-Cats, but lost the game and failed to qualify for the playoffs for the first time since 2005.

Like any high level executive, Bauer believed he needed the authority to make decisions in the best interest of the team, without interference from the board. He knew he had to answer to the board and if they don't like the way he's doing things, they're free to fire him. But the everyday business of running the team, like hiring coaches and trading players, had to be handled by someone who understood the entire business. And that wasn't happening.

"Lyle knew what he was doing," said CJOB's Bob Irving. "He pulled the club out from the brink of disaster and he was the one who set the new stadium idea in motion. We wouldn't have a new stadium, let alone a team, if it wasn't for him."

Rumours started floating that he was a candidate for the vacant president's position with the Calgary Stampeders.

"I've always said, be careful what you ask me to do, because I will," said Bauer. "Regardless of who or what gets in the way. I'll may ruffle some feathers and kick some ass along the way, but I'll get it done."

"To be honest, the wheels were already in motion for me to leave and go to Calgary," said Bauer. "The board wasn't going to continue with Mike because he wasn't one to fall in line either. Mike was a good guy, but he wasn't one to kiss the media's ass. There were several Board members that loved the media and they liked being seen as the boss of the club."

"Lyle and I will always have mutual respect and we could and can speak frankly, without either one letting their feelings get in the way," said Mike Kelly. "Business was business, and it didn't interfere with our friendship and for that I will always be grateful because, quite frankly, it's difficult to find."

"He is supportive of his people and as the lunatic fringe gathered in 2009, I never felt like Lyle abandoned me," said Kelly. "I didn't make his life easy, but he stood by me, and for that I am thankful. He provided me with the opportunity I coveted most in my career, to be the Head Coach of the Winnipeg Blue Bombers."

"There was also a change in chairman coming," recalls Bauer. "In the past, I was fortunate to have some great chairman to work with in Ken Hildahl, Gene Dunn, and David Asper. I had also worked with other past presidents (before the implementation of the chairman position) and board members that were also excellent. Ted Bartman, Bruce Robinson, Reg Low, Ross Brown, Murdoch McKay, Blake Fitzpatrick, Ken Houssin, Brock Bulbuck, Harry Ethans, Barry Loudon and Bob Miles were all top notch people who helped guide the team."

"The previous chairmen had set a very high standard which I believed in," said Bauer. "But I had a feeling the incoming chair wasn't a fan of mine, so the writing was on the wall. Also, remember at that time, there was a faction that was trying desperately to give Asper the club."

"I should probably explain my personal stand a little better," said Bauer. "As a preface, the CFL is a very 'distinct entity.'"

"The CFL has survived many times in spite of itself and in order to continue, there has to be a balance in ownership; community owned clubs and private," said Bauer. "As I've said before, there would be no league without Winnipeg, Saskatchewan and Edmonton. They have supported the private mismanaged teams for years, in particular during the late 70s, 80s, and 90s. Winnipeg and Saskatchewan have had their struggles, but that can be attributed to the bailing out of the CFL and other clubs."

"I firmly believed that the Blue Bombers should remain under public ownership," said Bauer. "But there was a faction of the board that were determined to turn the club over to David Asper."

"We were in the middle of trying to get a new stadium for the team, but I also knew that the numbers being thrown around were not realistic. They were at least $100mm short."

"We had experience in doing this when we worked with Leo Ledohowski and Canad Inns when we had a plan to build an enclosed stadium with attached trade/convention space, a hotel, shopping, etc. I still to this day believe that would have been the best for Winnipeg and the province. It would have opened new markets and opportunities. But, unfortunately, it was before it's time and we couldn't get support from the city or the province. In hindsight, for what they had to contribute and will contribute for the existing stadium, it would have been a much better investment."

"There was a game back in the mid-eighties that I remember," said Bauer. "We were playing in Montreal and the game was tight. We were close to scoring for the win but I went offside and we gave up the ball."

"I walked back to the sidelines and Cal wouldn't even look at me. He was so disappointed in me. I knew I had let him and the team down. After the game, he wouldn't talk to me. He ignored me on the flight home and for the next few days at practice. It was tearing me up. I couldn't shake that feeling."

"Finally, two days later, after practice, I walked up to him and said, 'Can we please get this over with?' He just looked at me and laughed. Then, without saying a word, he walked away."

"Cal knew that the disappointment had been gnawing away inside of me and that was more than enough of a punishment. He didn't have to do or say anything more."

"When I was on that line, I knew my job. I knew what my responsibilities were and I was damn good at them. But, as an executive, when there isn't alignment between the board and management it's hard to succeed. The growing fear of disappointing the team and the fans becomes a motivating factor. I knew the pitfalls of what was to come. In best case situations you have two choices; abandon your beliefs and plans, and fall in line, or maintain them. Obviously the latter was a major factor in my decision to leave. I knew my time with the Blue Bombers was coming to an end."

"When someone is at the top of their game, everybody wants to be a part of their social circle," said Brodie Bauer. "But in 2009, when my Dad resigned from the Blue Bombers, I felt anger from the community. It was almost as though the Bauer's had become the scapegoat for the problems with the Winnipeg Blue Bombers."

"When my Dad announced he was going to work with Stampeders, I was still in Winnipeg," said Danni. "I remember him and I went to get my oil changed. There was a copy of the newspaper there and he was on the cover with the words, 'Traitor.'"

"I learned a lot from that," said Brodie. "Who I can trust and who I cannot. There were a lot of people who I never saw again after my Dad left the Blue Bombers, and a lot of them I thought were close friends with the family. If anything this opened my eyes to the ugly side of professional sports and also the ugly side of people."

"I was proud of what we had accomplished," said Bauer. "The Winnipeg Blue Bombers were financially stable and the team's future looked pretty good. But, there was still something weighing on me. Every day I was getting more and more phone calls and messages from people being affected by cancer."

Chapter Fifteen

On December 16, 2009, Lyle Bauer resigned as President and CEO of the Winnipeg Football Club. Twenty-four hours later, the board of directors fired head coach, Mike Kelly.

Under his leadership, Bauer had led the Winnipeg Blue Bombers to a 90-88-2 record. The team had made the postseason seven of the ten seasons and advanced to the Grey Cup in 2001 and 2007. The club hosted five playoff games and one Grey Cup.

He had taken over the franchise in 2000 when the football club was more than $5 million in debt. He immediately set out to implement a strategic business plan that would guide the club on the path to success and establish a model where the community and fans once again felt proud of the Blue Bombers.

Twenty- two days after resigning from the Winnipeg Football Club, the Calgary Stampeders announced Lyle Bauer as the club's new president.

John Forzani, the managing partner of business operations for the Stampeders had posted a statement on their website stating, "Lyle brings tremendous administration skills to the Stampeders and we're excited about having him take control of the club's business operations. He did an exceptional job of turning around the Winnipeg Blue Bombers' financial situation and has also been very successful in his non-football business pursuits."

"In Calgary, there was an upstart group of private owners," said Bauer. "It was led by Ted Hellard and John Forzani. That group was very interesting and also included a small ownership percentage from Murray Edwards and the Calgary Flames."

Bauer would oversee and operate all of the Stampeders' business operations, while former teammate John Hufnagel continued as general manager and head coach.

"That was an exciting opportunity," said Bauer. "The other attraction in going to Calgary was that I would get to work with John Hufnagel who was a former teammate of mine and who I thought was the best in the business. I had always wanted to hire Huff, but never had the resources to get him."

Hufnagel had spent three and half years with the Blue Bombers, before being traded to Saskatchewan in 1987, where he began his coaching career as a player-coach for the Roughriders. From 1990–1996 Hufnagel was the offensive coordinator for the Calgary Stampeders.

He spent the 2003 season with the Super Bowl champion New England Patriots, where under Hufnagel's guidance, Tom Brady earned his second Super Bowl MVP award.

In 2008, Hufnagel stepped in as the Calgary head coach and the Stampeders ended their playoff victory drought and won the team's sixth Grey Cup in a 22–14 victory over the Montreal Alouettes.

"I first met Lyle when I was traded from Saskatchewan to Winnipeg midway thru the 1983 season," said Hufnagel. "I remember Lyle on several occasions having to save my ass from the wrath of Chis Walby because of my teasing."

"I really wasn't aware of Lyle's cancer problem until I came back to coach the Stampeders in 2008 and he became President of The Stamps," said Hufnagel. "We had numerous discussions about his ordeal."

"Over the years I watched the commitment the Calgary ownership group had demonstrated to ensure the viability of this organization for the city, their fans, staff and players," said Bauer. "They also had a commitment to acquire the best talent, on and off the field."

"Calgary was also responsible for helping me get a scholarship in the United States. Former Assistant General Manager, Joe Tiller, helped me get that opportunity and that started my road to the CFL. So I guess there was a part of me that wanted to give back to that club as well."

Bauer set out on his new assignment with the same vigour and tenacity he had applied in Winnipeg. "The Stampeders wanted to continue to improve their business on and off the field," said Bauer. "We also wanted to expand into having concerts, running the stadium, and maybe acquiring other sports entities."

"We did a business plan, which would see the organization enter into new business opportunities and take over the refurbishment of McMahon Stadium as well as taking over the stadium's operations. It was the same template as what we did in Winnipeg."

In his first year with the team, the Calgary Stampeders finished the 2010 season in 1st place in the West division with a 13–5 record.

They attempted to win their 7th Grey Cup championship, but lost in the West Final.

In 2011, they finished in 3rd place in the West division with an 11–7 record and lost the West Semi-Final game to the Edmonton Eskimos.

In 2012, the Stampeders finished in 2nd place in the West Division with a 12–6 record. They won the West Semi-Final over the Saskatchewan Roughriders by a score of 36–30. It was the team's first playoff victory over Saskatchewan since 1994.

The team then traveled to Vancouver and upset the 1st place B.C. Lions 34–29, and advanced to the Grey Cup game. They went into the Grey Cup as favourites, but lost 35–22 to the hometown Toronto Argonauts.

"The Calgary Flames had part ownership of the Stampeders and both organizations had the same basic business philosophy," said Bauer. "Eventually the Flames stepped up to buy out the remaining partners of the football operations and set out to expand and create their own empire."

"I assisted them in the transition and helped streamline the operation," said Bauer. "When the transition was complete, they offered me the opportunity to stay, however it was clear that Ken King and I were very similar and that probably wouldn't have worked out well for me. I elected to leave and left on good terms, wishing them the best."

So on January 23, 2013, after three successful years as the team's president and chief operating officer, Bauer announced his resignation.

After 27 years of playing and management experience in the CFL, Bauer decided to join a team that had come to be near and dear to his heart.

"A big part of leaving Calgary was the Never Alone Foundation," said Bauer. "It was becoming very difficult meeting the obligations that I had set out for the foundation while being in Calgary. There was a pull to help those people that were fighting against cancer. I needed to be there to support the staff and volunteers. Leaving allowed me to heed that calling and focus on the true battle."

"And remember, I don't lose."

Chapter Sixteen

Webster's defines the term generosity as: *the quality of being kind, understanding, and not selfish.*

Generosity is an act that can change the world. It works its magic one person at a time; then, almost effortlessly, its multiplying force animates families, friends, communities, cultures, and the world at large.

In short, generosity inspires generosity.

Lyle Bauer still remembers the day he was drafted into the CFL. He has vivid memories of the moment his hand, as a champion, first touched the Grey Cup. He remembers those precious moments when he first looked into the eyes of his three children. But he can't recall the moment he was informed that he had cancer.

"I was alone in that moment," said Bauer. "Heidi was there, but she wasn't. Dr. Sutherland was in the room, but I didn't see her. It was just me, wondering, what's next."

But the support and generosity he received from family, friends, strangers and cancer service providers that stepped in alongside him, let him know that he was not alone.

"His recovery was really a miracle when you think about it," said Debra Lofvendahl. "I believe Lyle's courage and strength to survive was not just for himself and his family, but to help others going through the same fight to never feel alone. That's how and why The Never Alone Foundation was established."

Bauer started forming the Never Alone Foundation in early 2005 while he was still undergoing his own treatment. In the beginning he pulled together people he knew could get the ball rolling and who knew what his vision was. He called on Gene Dunn, Ken Hildahl and others to help set up the foundation.

"Jerry Maslowsky was there from the very beginning. He was there when I was going through treatments and was always there to lend a hand," Bauer said of the former Blue Bomber Sales and Marketing Manager. "If your life is measured by the difference you make in the lives of others then Jerry is definitely at the top of the class."

"We spent so much time pouring our hearts into that club together," said Bauer. "His passion for the Blue and Gold was unparalleled. His knowledge, conviction, passion and friendship are things I will never forget.   I am truly sorry that we were not able to deliver him and his family a Grey Cup Championship and ring."

In 2005, Shirlee Preteau was the vice president of the Winnipeg Blue Bombers Facilities and Events Operations. She is now the Director of Fund Development for the Foundation. "Lyle's passion was infectious," she recalls. "We all wanted to help him."

"The first event we did was the 2005 CFL Coach of the Year Award," said Shirlee." And things just took off from there."

Today, the Never Alone Foundation supports numerous programs in an effort to ensure that victims of cancer are never alone in their battle. From revitalizing the rooms of a palliative care unit to providing funds to stage a puppet program to explain the effects of cancer to children, the Bauer's Never Alone Foundation strives to make a difference in the lives of cancer patients and their families. The Foundation provides gift baskets, food and gas gift certificates, books, and advice on who to contact for other services. And more importantly, to simply lend an ear or the opportunity to talk with someone who has gone through this same journey.

"My father is a very caring and giving man," said daughter, Danni. "I think that is something that has been passed on to Brodie and Wesley and myself."

"When I was in high school, I felt nobody truly understood what our family was going through," said Wesley Bauer. "I remember the first day all of Winnipeg found out. I was lying in the back seat of Dad's truck and Bob Irving came on the radio and said, 'Lyle Bauer has been diagnosed with cancer.' And then it was in the paper and right away I thought, great, now every single person in my life knows about our family's personal life."

"Initially, that was hard for us," Wesley continued. "I think we pushed our emotions aside and for me, I never talked about it. I thought if I ignored it, it would simply go away. I remember a good friend approaching me and asking me why I never talked about my Dad's diagnosis. I replied, 'I just don't want to.'"

"But I watched my father take a completely different approach. He took everything head on. He continued doing his job at the Winnipeg Blue Bomber's office and eventually turned his diagnosis into something positive. I think as a family that taught us a lot."

His father's approach to the disease and treatment eventually become an inspiration for Wesley. "Wes called me one day and said he wanted to take a year off to train to do something special," said Lyle. "He wanted to ride a bike across Canada to raise money for the foundation. He was going to school in B.C. at the time. I told him no."

"I will never forget calling my father and telling him I was not going back to college and him telling me that I was. I told him I wanted to cycle across Canada to raise money for the Never Alone Foundation," said Wesley. "At that point he threw all of his support behind me." And Chase the Cure was born.

Wes became a young man on a mission; a mission to do his part to help bring awareness and to support education in cancer research.

Chase the Cure would start in Victoria, B.C. on May 14, 2009 and ended in St. John's, Newfoundland. With the help of friends, Al Moffat, Phil Wilson and Susan Faso, they were able to arrange the use of an RV. Jim White of Signcraft Display provided the wrap for the vehicle. Bauer's other son Brodie would follow his brother in the RV across the country.

"I remember driving Wes and Brodie to Victoria to start them off," said Lyle. "It was very stressful turning our boys loose."

"To see our kids take a stand and want to do something to help people was a pretty powerful message," said Heidi. "I've heard it said that there are lessons to be learned with cancer and it's true."

"Cancer is horrible," Heidi continued. "But Chase the Cure became very important to our family. Lyle set up The Never Alone Foundation to help others, but Chase the Cure was meant to help us."

"I realized that although cancer has a way of humbling anyone and putting life in perspective, it makes you realize the importance of memories," said Wesley. "It makes you realize the importance of being there for family, friends and even a stranger in need. Chase the Cure would embody that lesson for my family. As a 20 year old, I didn't realize what it truly meant. It really was important for my family. It gave us an opportunity to band together and the example my Father was setting by turning something negative into something beneficial for society."

"It felt natural for me to do it," said Wes. "I had the support from everybody. My sister was involved and my brother drove the RV behind me the entire summer. When the ride was over, we had talked to over 100 media outlets. Every CFL team welcomed us and we raised over $100,000 for the Never Alone Foundation."

"But more than the money, the neat thing for us as a family was it showed us how many friends we had supporting us," said Wes. "They came in droves to ensure that the ride was a success. It just reiterated to me no matter what you are going through in life, there is someone out there who understands. It takes courage to be there, but you have a duty to show that person they are never alone."

"There are so many people that don't have a back-up," said Lyle. "That person to be there to drive them to appointments. To take care of them. To ask the questions when they're in no position to do that."

"That's part of what the foundation is there for," said Bauer. "Our purpose is to be there for people. To talk to them, hold their hand. Send them a blanket or a fruit basket."

"There's no policy book to this whole thing," said Michael Schiefer, Executive Director of the Never Alone Foundation. "If there's a need we do our best to fill it."

"Lyle is definitely the driving force behind what we do," said Shirley It's not 'if' or 'how can we do it,' it's 'we must do it.'"

"When Lyle heard that Steve Rodehutkors, a former linemate was ill, we made arrangements to bring him and his family from Calgary to Winnipeg to watch the Grey Cup game," said Shirlee.

"When Tyrone Jones, another former teammate was battling his cancer in the United States, Lyle and the Foundation found a way to help cover some of his treatments."

"There are so many needs those patients have that aren't covered," said Shirlee. "Compression garments for lymphedema support for example, are extremely expensive, but they're essential to a patient's needs. We help with those."

"Ray went down the same path as Lyle," said Marcia Davis. In 2008, Marcia's husband Ray was diagnosed with Stage 4 throat cancer, similar to Bauer's. "I don't remember how the initial connection was made, but Ray was so excited when he told me Lyle Bauer had called him. It made all the difference in the world to him."

"When I would come home from work, I could always tell when Lyle had called Ray. He was always a little brighter."

"It's hard on this journey to not get whisked away by the darkness and go down a spiral of depression," said Shianne, a Never Alone client. "The truth is, you need to get up and fight for the life you want to live. The Never Alone Foundation is more than a foundation, it is family. The people working there are absolutely amazing. Never too busy for you, ready to listen, laugh, cry and hug at the drop of a hat. They make this crappy journey more tolerable."

"I feel like it's part of the debt I owe," said Bauer. "When you fight cancer and beat it, you get touched by the support of so many, you want to pay that forward by helping others. I had to do something to try and make a difference for others who are facing their own battles. Sometimes it's just a phone call or a note, other times it's a hospital visit."

"The heart and soul contributions come in the form of simple, but priceless acts," said Bauer. "Comfort blankets for someone in the hospital, parking and transportation funds for families who have extensive costs while their loved one is going through treatment."

"We've done a weekend away for a couple who both have cancer so they could forget their fight for a few hours. We've provided a family vacation for a mother and her young sons to help deal with the loss of her husband and their father," Bauer continued.

Bauer will be the first to admit, he doesn't have all the answers when it comes to cancer. In most cases, it's all about listening, about providing a shoulder to cry on or information on what services may be available to help in the fight. Despite the damage from his own treatment, Bauer's voice is still powerful, because he's lived through it all.

When the foundation out grew their original office space, Kevin Klein, the publisher of the Winnipeg Sun in 2009 stepped up. He offered Lyle and the foundation space in their building.

"It had nothing to do with the Blue Bombers," said Klein. "It was the socially responsible thing to do. Lyle and the foundation were on the frontlines, helping those in need. They weren't just raising money for a cause, they are actively making a difference."

"That tremendous support continues today," said Bauer. "Thanks to Daria Zmiyiwsky, the current publisher of the Winnipeg Sun.

"Lyle was key in getting the Dental Support Program established," said Tom Scott, another throat cancer survivor whose journey crossed with Bauer's.

"People don't realize that in some cases your teeth can be damaged during treatments," said Scott. "Dental reconstruction is not covered and most benefit plans don't come close to covering the cost."

"Just imagine having battled this horrible disease and coming out on the other side with no teeth. You have to eat your dinner through a straw. That's just not acceptable."

"We provided the means for new dental work for a cancer patient who had significant oral damage from her treatments. She was able to smile and face the world again."

Oral cancer is the largest group of those cancers which fall into the head and neck cancer category. In 2016, approximately 4,600 people in Canada were diagnosed with oral cancer.

"Unfortunately, the majority are found as late stage cancers," said Scott, who volunteers with the Foundation. Late stage diagnosis is occurring because most of these cancers are hard to discover and also because of a lack of public awareness.

Scott, and the Never Alone Foundation, in partnership with The Manitoba Dental Association and Sirius Benefits Plan, now hold a free Oral Cancer Screening clinic at Polo Park Mall every April.

"Don't forget, as much as a patient goes through it, the family goes through it as well," said Bauer. "We can't forget the impact it has on them."

"My Dad has Stage 4 lung cancer," said Shannon B, another Never Alone client. "This has been the hardest time in our lives. The Never Alone Foundation has given us a helping hand when we needed it the most. Giving my parents a break away to spend time together, giving my Dad a garden that he can spend his last months in and giving us all hope we are not alone in all this."

"I moved back to Canada from Scotland with my 2 year-old to take care of my Dad, leaving my husband behind in Scotland to work," Shannon continued. "We had been apart for eight months and when he came to visit, the Foundation let us stay at the Victoria Inn to spend time together."

"There are little things that people sometimes don't think about when they are completely focused on their fight against cancer," said Michael, who has been with the Foundation, first as a volunteer and now the Executive Director.

His first introduction to Lyle Bauer was a clear indication of who the man was. "I went to Shirley's home one evening," recalls Schiefer. "Lyle was still the President of the Blue Bombers and I had recently been to a game. I made the mistake of complaining that the windows at the stadium were dirty."

"Well, Lyle being Lyle, he told me to clean them. The next thing I knew, I was working at the stadium as a facility manager."

"One case this year was a family who wanted to go to the Red River Ex," said Schiefer. "We got them tickets, that part was easy. But you can't go to the Ex without enjoying a ride and taking in some of the food. We provided them with enough so that they could have a good time and forget the fight they were going through for a while."

"The needs that we uncover sometimes come from the relationships we've made over the past twelve years," said Michael. "In some cases, our volunteers will let us know what's needed. Most of them have been clients or had family members who have been involved with someone who has fought cancer."

"I've spent a lot of time with a lot of fabulous people," said Bauer. "Some have had bigger fights than I had and some of them lost theirs. My heart goes out to them every day."

"But we fight for a reason," said Bauer. "We fight for those who have gone before us. We fight for those who are fighting now. We will continue to fight for those who are coming after us to let them know that there's always help. There's always support. One thing about our people, no matter the request, no matter what is needed; we find a way to get it done."

"I think one of the biggest things that I realized especially after my Dad's battle with cancer was that what defines us as human beings is not what we do when everything is going smoothly," said Wesley. "It's how we overcome the obstacles and the imperfections that life throws our way that really define who are. My father had never let losing a football game or even cancer define who he was. To this day, he lets his day to day interactions and his compassion for others define him."

"As a 16 year-old boy watching his hero in a weak moment, overcoming the biggest fight of his life with such grace and compassion says it all," said Wesley. "As a family, he taught us how we should treat everyone no matter who they are. And for me, it all boiled down to treating others how my father treats them; with love, compassion and kindness."

"I owe Lyle and the Foundation so much," said Marcia Davies. "My husband is now gone, but the Foundation remains as close as family. I still volunteer at the events as my way saying thank you. My time and money will always go to support the Never Alone Foundation because it's the right thing to do. Because Lyle Bauer is such an inspiration. He truly is my cancer hero."

The Brothers

I am an only child with no siblings, but I do have a bunch of brothers that would do anything for each other. That is the special bond we have.

We shared the ups, downs, fights, victories, and losses. But we always had each other's back no matter the personalities, squabbles, or other issues that surface with any family environment.

Brothers forever.

David Black

What can I say about Blackie.   From a player standpoint, he was a very good athlete and a smart one. He has always been there as a great friend and when I wanted someone to be the Co-Chair of the Foundation, he was the logical choice.   Always has my back in so many ways. The type of person that you know you can count on no matter what, on and off the field.

Chris Walby

"Bluto" was my roommate for most of my 10 years with the club. Had some great times.   Used to try and scare the shit out of each other.....hid in shower and shit like that. He is probably the most dominant lineman I ever saw. He really should have been in the NFL. Again a great friend and loyal companion.

Bob Molle
"Bubs" was someone I knew from Saskatoon and played against his brother. Bob worked hard, didn't let pain stop him, and he was always yapping. Good soldier.

Steve Rodehutskors
"Rodie" was never a big fan of mine, but always a solid team guy. Great athlete......basketball player in university. He was smart as shit.....very cerebral and knew science, trivia, etc......and rather opinionated. We got along much better when he was diagnosed as he realized I had his back.

James West and Tyrone Jones
I can't talk about one without the other. They were joined at the hip and the lip. Obviously crazy talents. Ty and I had another bond, both of us had throat cancer. The Foundation was honoured to help him during his fight.

James is my brother. We didn't always agree, but we were united in our team. We have grown closer over the years and JW brings a spiritual conviction that is contagious. I couldn't have a asked for a better brother in my corner.

John Bonk
"J.B." was always funny, practical joker, and heck of an athlete. Undersized for a center in the latter years but did everything including long snapping. We supported him and his wife Chris when she was diagnosed with brain cancer and she has recovered. Man of strong faith and we were very close during our time together.

Stan Mikowas
"Stauch" never got the recognition he should have received for how good he was. As a nose guard you sacrifice yourself in every play so the ends and linebackers

can make plays......strong as shit and really a bitch to protect against daily.

Nick Bastaja
"Nick". Just called him by his name. Probably one of the scariest men you would ever meet in uniform. Had arms like tree trunks and very intense. Good guy

Rod Hill
Wow. He is something else. One of the most gifted corners you could ever find and he delivered game in and game out. His motor always runs and is tied to him mouth. Now I say that in a respectful manner. Rod says what he feels and means what he says. Great team guy and great friend. Has always been there on and off the field.

Nick Benjamin
Man, Nick was an athlete. Strong, fast, and a great guy who died way too young. I spoke at his funeral and that was a tough one.

I remember when Nick was with Ottawa and chased down David Shaw on an interception. Probably 80 yards and stopped Shaw from getting a touchdown. Nick also had the most distinctive laugh you could ever imagine......came right from the depths of his belly. Funny man.

As a national registered charity,
the Never Alone Foundation has the flexibility
to support many worthwhile agencies, projects and
programs that aid in the fight against cancer.
For more information or to make a donation to
The Never Alone Foundation, please call 204-779-2441